Rose Nimmo Engelhardt
The Story of Rose and Her Family

Barbara L. Hunter

KOLBURY PRESS
Rose Nimmo Engelhardt: The Story of Rose and Her Family
Barbara L. Hunter

Copyright © 2018 Barbara L. Hunter
All rights reserved.
ISBN 10: 0-9884208-8-0
ISBN 13: 978-0-9884208-8-5
Library of Congress Control Number: 2018946901

Published by: Kolbury Press

Printed in the United States of America

FOR MY AUNT, ROSE NIMMO ENGELHARDT
WITH GRATITUDE AND LOVE

FOR MY DEAR COUSINS:
DOLORES ENGELHARDT ARDEN
AND
JANICE ENGELHARDT KOLLER

CONTENTS

ACKNOWLEDGMENTS

My Aunt Rose Marion Nimmo Engelhardt was always enthusiastic, loving, and supportive. With this book, I have tried to honor Rose and to recount the history of Rose and her family so subsequent generations can more fully understand and cherish their heritage.

Beth Koller Whittenbury, Rose's granddaughter, is a writer and publisher. Beth spent hours and days helping me develop and publish this book. Anyone interested in tackling a similar self-publishing project can get Beth's book, *How to Self Publish Your Book in Ten Easy Steps: A Guide for Authors Who Want Publish Their Books for Free* on Amazon. Or, Beth can be reached at her website, www.bethwhittenbury.com, or via email to beth@bethwhittenbury.com.

In the course of developing the book, Beth and I found that the book needed more material on Rose's early life. Using her mother's unpublished manuscripts, Beth wrote a major part of Chapter 6, "Rose - Early Days."

I couldn't have completed the book without the unwavering support of the "Rose Team" - Dolores Engelhardt Arden, Beth Koller Whittenbury and Sue Arden West. Their memories and photographs made Rose and her family come alive.

A big thanks to my Texas Feldtman family who have always been so supportive and welcoming when I've visited Texas.

This book has been enriched by fascinating family stories and diligent research from Jody Rippel Feldtman Wright, Fern Feldtman Fahnert, Sandy Fahnert Stacy, Gail Noonan Fordyce, George Caspar Feldtman, Jr., Katy Feldtman, Sheila Feldtman, Charles Rogers Wiseman and Tootie Simpson.

Cathy Feldtman Westberg shared family photos and stories, and, ultimately, generously gave me her father's family research and his Feldtman family correspondence. Liz Tice and Lou Nelson of the Willamette Valley Genealogical Society helped me climb over the many genealogical "brick walls." My thanks to Bill Lenzke for enormous amounts of computer help. Thanks to Elysia DeLaurentis, Pat Adam and Gina Dewaele of Ontario, Canada for invaluable research on the Nimmo's time in Ontario. Sheri Fenley found genealogical gems on the Manns and the Eichenbergers during the time they lived in San Joaquin County, California. Thanks to JoAnn Elizabeth Seibert and Ingrid Brandt for splendid translations of difficult "old" German writing. Margaret Loftis was an outstanding proofreader.

My citations of sources are simplified. However, much of the documentation can be found in my Ancestry Family Tree: "Hunter Wright Engelhardt Feldtman," - or it is in my possession. I can be reached at: hunterbl1@comcast.net.

All mistakes are my own. BLH

"Thank you so much all of you who contributed to making this book so special for all of us –" Dolores Engelhardt Arden, Rose's daughter.

1
TWIN HOUSES

"They stood through the 1906 quake, and they are still there." Janice Engelhardt Koller

From the time she was 2 years old in 1905 until she married in 1925, Rose Marion Nimmo lived with her family in one of the twin Victorian houses on Buena Vista Avenue in San Francisco.[1] [2]

The horseshoe shaped Buena Vista Avenue begins at Haight Street with its neighborhood shops and churches. It curves up a steep hillside, around the beautiful 36-acre Buena Vista Park[3] that covers the very top of the hill,[4]

---

[1] George and Lena Nimmo, their son, Tom, and their daughter, Rose, lived at 485 Buena Vista Avenue in San Francisco. Rose's grandmother, Rosa Schnepple and various uncles lived next door at 483 Buena Vista Avenue.

[2] The houses were built on lots in the Flint Tract which was surveyed by Wm. P. Humphreys in 1867. In: "Map of the Lands of the Flint Tract Homestead Association / surveyed by Wm. P/ Humphreys." In: http://hdl.huntington.org/cdm/printview/collection" database entry for "Flint Tract." (Accessed: 13 Mar 2018)

[3] Buena Vista Park was the first park established in San Francisco. When it was created in 1867, it was called Hill Park. Later the name was changed to Buena Vista. "Buena Vista Park." *Wikipedia*. 2016.

[4] In the early days, the city had reserved the areas at tops of the hills for livestock grazing which is why the crowns of the San Francisco hills remain "clear" to this day. Louis M. Hunter: as told to his daughter, Barbara Hunter.

and then descends the other side of the hill - back to Haight Street.

The twin homes are perched right at the top of Buena Vista Avenue. From the front of their house, the Nimmo family could see a "perfect" view of Buena Vista Park just across the street. From the back of the twin houses, the family had a spectacular view of the city.

Imagine - a breathtaking view on one side and an enticing park on the other - twin reasons to build twin homes on Buena Vista.

The "twin" homes of the Nimmo family: 483 and 485 Buena Vista Avenue, Buena Vista Heights, San Francisco, California. Before 1925. Courtesy of Dolores Arden.

Both Nimmo homes were built in 1904[5] [6] by Rose's father, George Nimmo, a San Francisco carpenter and building contractor.[7] [8] They are still

---

[5] In March of 1904, George Schnepple, Rose's uncle, bought 2 lots (lots 8 and 9, block 6, Flint Tract Homestead) in San Francisco for $10. In: *San Francisco Call* (San Francisco, California), Sat, Mar 5, 1904. Pp. 14. (newspaper notice) *Newspapers.com* database entry for George Schnepple.

[6] By April of 1904, George Schnepple had contracted with George Nimmo, Rose's father, to build two one-story cottages on these lots (the lots described in the prior footnote) for $4000. In: *San Francisco Call* (San Francisco, California), Sat, Apr 9, 1904. Pp. 14. (newspaper notice) *Newspapers.com* database entry for George Schnepple.

[7] George Nimmo built both houses. Family history recounted by Dolores Engelhardt Arden, George's granddaughter.

[8] George Nimmo and his family lived at 2208 Larkin Street in 1904 and 485 Buena Vista in 1905. In: "San Francisco City Directory, 1904, 1905," *Ancestry.com* database entry for George Nimmo. The Schnepples may have moved in first as they were living at 483 Buena Vista in 1904. In: "San Francisco City Directory, 1903, 1904," *Ancestry.com* database entry for George Schnepple.

pleasing to look at as they were built in the recognizable Victorian style so typical of turn-of-the-twentieth-century San Francisco.[9]

Rose lived in the larger of the two houses[10] with her father, George Nimmo, her mother, Lena Schnepple Nimmo, and her older brother, Tom.[11]

The Nimmos: Lena, Tom, George and Rose.
San Francisco, California. About 1915.
Courtesy of Dolores Engelhardt Arden.

Rose's grandmother, Rosa Eichenberger Schnepple, and some of Rose's Schnepple uncles lived next door in the other house at 483 Buena Vista Avenue. Rosa Schnepple, of course, was Lena Schnepple Nimmo's mother.

---

[9] The architect was C. S. McNally. In: *San Francisco Call* (San Francisco, California) Sat, Apr 9, 1904. Pp. 14. (newspaper notice) *Newspapers.com* database entry for George Schnepple.

[10] 485 Buena Vista Avenue is the house to the right as you face the two houses.

[11] "1910 United States Federal Census," *Ancestry.com* database entry for George Nimmo.

Three Generations: Rosa Eichenberger Schnepple, Lena Schnepple Nimmo and Dolores Engelhardt. San Francisco. Courtesy of Dolores Engelhardt Arden.

Uncle Fred Schnepple and Rose Nimmo. San Francisco. About 1915. Courtesy of Dolores Engelhardt Arden.

George Schnepple, the oldest of the Schnepple uncles, always lived with his mother. The other uncles - Ernst, Robert and Frederick[12] - generally lived with their mother, Rosa Eichenburger Schnepple, until they were married.[13] [14]

***

---

[12] "Ernst" became "Ernest" and "Frederick" called himself "Frank."

[13] "San Francisco, California, City Directories, 1896-1924," *Ancestry.com* database entries for Rosa Schnepple, George Schnepple, Robert Schnepple, Ernest Schnepple and Frederick Schnepple. "Oakland City Directories, 1925-1942," *Ancestry.com* database entry for Rosa Schnepple, George Schnepple, Robert Schnepple, Ernest Schnepple and Frederick Schnepple. "1924, California Voter Registrations." *Ancestry.com* database entry for George Schnepple.

[14] "1910, United States Federal Census." *Ancestry.com* database entry for Rosa Schnepple.

Rose's house had three levels: the main floor, the attic, and the basement. From the street level, you climbed a flight of stairs to the front door which opened onto an entry hall.

On your right, off the entry hall, was the front parlor. Right behind the parlor was a small room where George, Rose's father, had his bed. Rose's mother, Lena, had the back bedroom. Rose and her brother, Tom, slept in the attic.

To the left side of the entry hall, on the main floor, George Nimmo built a completely enclosed "corridor" between the two homes, so his mother-in-law, Rosa, could walk between the houses without going outside. There were doors at either end of the corridor to enter and exit each residence.[15]

If you came into the entry hall and then went straight ahead, you would pass a hall tree and a small table that held the family telephone, and you would enter the family dining room. Behind the dining room was the kitchen and a single bath.[16] The back porch was just off the kitchen. Very steep stairs led to the back yard.

The dining room had a beautiful oak table – "to kill for." Near the window in the dining room, George Nimmo would sit and relax in his favorite chair.

The kitchen had a wooden drain board, a big bin table where Lena kept her flour and sugar, and a cooler – but no refrigerator. The day before Thanksgiving, Lena - sometimes with the help of her daughter, Rose, and sometimes with the help of her granddaughters, Doll and Jannie - would prepare the turkey - complete with "old fashioned stuffing." Once the turkey was stuffed, it was left in a cooler on the back porch overnight. It was cooked the next day. When the Thanksgiving dinner was over, the

---

[15] Beth Koller Whittenbury and Dolores Engelhardt Arden: story told to Barbara Hunter.

[16] "As for the layout of the house - go up the front stairs - straight ahead is a hall - to the right as you exit the stairs - inside is a living room facing the street - George's bed was in the next room and Lena's bedroom (was) next. Going back to the hall, if you go straight ahead you land in the dining room (having passed on the left in the hall the small pass way to Nana's house). The dining room leads to the kitchen and the single bathroom. Lena's bedroom also had a door to the dining room. Simple arrangement. Upstairs was Tom and Rose's bedrooms - Hope this helps. Hugs, Doll." Dolores Engelhardt Arden: email to Beth Koller. (7 Mar 2018)

"guys" played pinochle in the dining room, and "mother" did the dishes.[17]

The delicious recipe for the turkey stuffing continues to be passed down through the family. According to Lena's great-granddaughter, Susan Arden West, this is Great-Grandma Lena's recipe:

Great-Grandma Lena's Stuffing Recipe[18]

"Tear up bread (any kind) 3 days before you make the stuffing and let it sit out to dry.

The day before you stuff the turkey:

Chop yellow onion and celery (lots) & sauté in butter.
In separate pan, brown sausage (lots). Pour onto paper towel to remove excess oil.

Meanwhile season the dried bread with pepper & lots of poultry seasoning.

Beat several eggs & pour onto bread.

Add 1 stick of melted butter and/or broth. You determine how much butter; eggs & broth are to be used to get correct consistency. You want the dried bread very damp but not too mushy.

Add celery, onion & sausage mixture & toss. Continue to toss & add **more seasoning** & liquid as needed.

Put into a container & store in refrigerator until you stuff the turkey.[19]

The morning you cook the turkey – stuff with above. Yummy & delicious!!

---

[17] All of the descriptions of the house and events from Rose's daughter, Dolores Engelhardt Arden in emails and phone calls to Barbara Hunter.

[18] West, Susan Arden. "Great-Grandma Lena's Stuffing Recipe." Susan Arden West: an email to Barbara Hunter.

[19] Note: This is the modern version of the recipe in which you store the stuffing in the refrigerator instead of storing the stuffed turkey in the "cooler" on the back porch - overnight.

***

George and Lena's home "always had a feeling of coziness. It was furnished simply and was very comfortable."[20] These well-built houses, containing the stories of two families, still stand today - as handsome and as sturdy as ever.

***

Rose's daughter, Dolores Engelhardt Arden, remembers her grandparents, George and Lena Nimmo, very well:

"I remember George's (my grandfather's) carpenter shop - it was on upper Montgomery (Street) on a slight hill and next to an alley I think. I spent enough time there that I can remember playing (using the paper 'curls' that grandpa shaved off his wood etc.)."[21] [22]

George Nimmo's Carpenter Shop on Montgomery Street, San Francisco, California. About 1950.

Courtesy of Beth Koller Whittenbury.

---

[20] Dolores Engelhardt Arden: an email to Barbara Hunter. (10 Nov 2107)

[21] When Dolores played there, the carpenter shop was at 804 Montgomery Street, San Francisco, California. In: "San Francisco, California, City Directory, 1937." *Ancestry.com* database entry for George Nimmo. (Accessed: 9 Jan 2013)

[22] Dolores Engelhardt Arden: an email to Barbara Hunter.

"Grandma Nimmo (Lena) did the 'books' for the shop (long before women did that sort of a thing) - Grandpa constructed everything from the 2 houses to making frames for the starving artists at the time - He made cabinets and all sorts of things. There was a basement and when wood was delivered they would open a door at the front of the building and slide the wood down to the basement."

"Something I remember about him and I have to smile because he was a true "scot" - however whenever we went to his home on Buena Vista Ave. and got ready to leave, he always gave Jannie and me a beautiful shiny silver dollar - that was such a treat - he would sit in 'his' chair by the window and have a smile on his face and give us the dollars."

"He really was a hard worker as was she-"

***

"Grandma took me and Jannie and cousin Phyllis[23] to the World's Fair[24] - it was a big event and we would take the ferry boat and spend the day and my folks would pick us up at the ferry building and take us home - they could not afford to go because of the money situation."

"Grandma was little - under 5 feet and she would keep up with us and we saw many great and memorable things at the fair - I remember when we returned to SF at night we would stand at the back of the boat and watch the lovely lights at the fair…. They were really dear people."[25]

---

[23] Phillis Nimmo (1924-2004) was the daughter of Rose's brother, Thomas Nimmo, and his wife, Josephine Ferrero Nimmo.

[24] The 1939 World's Fair, Treasure Island on San Francisco Bay was reached by ferry boats from San Francisco's Embarcadero.

[25] Dolores Engelhardt Arden: email to Barbara Hunter. (17 Jan 2016)

L to R: Tom Nimmo, Dolores Engelhardt, Janice Engelhardt and Phillis Nimmo. At the "1939 Exposition," on Treasure Island in San Francisco Bay. Note: The girls were born 6 years apart: Phyllis in 1924, Dolores in 1930 and Janice in 1936.
Courtesy of Beth Koller Whittenbury.

Lena Schnepple Nimmo at 1939 "Exposition" on Treasure Island in San Francisco Bay.
Courtesy of Beth Koller Whittenbury.

BARBARA L. HUNTER

2
SCOTISH ROOTS
THE NIMMOS AND THE CHALMERS

Rose.
Courtesy of Beth Koller Whittenbury.

George Nimmo, Rose's father, must have acquired the skills to build his two beautiful Buena Vista homes quite naturally. As far back as credible research will take us, George's Scots ancestors were mostly carpenters, joiners and wrights.[26] That is, they were craftsmen who were able to earn a living for their large families by their ability to work with wood.

---

[26] A "wright" is someone who makes or builds objects out of wood.

The Nimmos – Direct Line[27]

Daughter	**Rose Nimmo**	1903	San Francisco, CA
Son	**Thomas Nimmo**	1901	San Francisco, CA
Parents	**George Nimmo**	1867	Kirkliston, Scotland
	m. Lena Schnepple	1876	San Francisco, CA
Grandparents	**Thomas Nimmo**	1844	Kirkliston, Scotland
	m. Marion Kerr		
	Chalmers	1845	Kirkliston, Scotland
Great	**David Nimmo**	1803	Abercorn, Scotland
Grandparents	m. Jean (Jane)		
	McGill (Magill)	1808	Keills, Scotland
2nd Great	**Matthew Nimmo**	1767	Abercorn, Scotland
Grandparents	m. Janet Davie	1769	Linlithgow, Scotland

Matthew Nimmo.[28] George Nimmo's great grandfather, Matthew Nimmo, was born on July 3, 1767.[29] He was listed as a "joiner" on the 1841 Scotland Census.[30] [31]

On September 1, 1795, Matthew Nimmo married Janet Davie in

---

[27] Hunter, Barbara L. "Rose Nimmo - Hunter Wright Engelhardt Feldtman." (Ancestry Family Tree), Owner: hunterbl175. *Ancestry.com* database.

[28] The "Hunter Wright Engelhardt Feldtman" tree on *Ancestry.com* has both the Nimmo and Chalmers line extending further back than is mentioned in this book. However, I'm currently not as certain that that genealogy is absolutely correct so I've not included the earlier Nimmo and Chalmers's lines here.

[29] "1841 Scotland Census." *Ancestry.com* database entry for Matthew Nimmo.

[30] Ibid. "1841 Scotland Census."

[31] A joiner is a person who joins wood together to make the wooden components of a building, such as window frames, stairs and doors. In: "joiner." *Wikipedia*. (19 Jan 2016)

Abercorn, West Lothian, Scotland.[32] They had 7 children including **David** Nimmo, George Nimmo's grandfather, who was born on September 22, 1803 in Abercorn.[33]

Children of Matthew Nimmo (1767) and Janet Davie (1769)[34]

1. Henry   1796
2. John   1798
3. John   1803
4. **David**   1803
5. Agnes   1806
6. Jannet (Janet) 1808
7. James   1811

David Nimmo. David Nimmo (b. 1803) was a joiner and a wright by profession.[35] A wright is a "worker skilled in the manufacture especially of wooden objects."[36] Either as a joiner or as a wright, David made a living for his family as a skilled woodworker.

David Nimmo married Jane (or "Jean") McGill (or "Magill") from Keills, Kirkbroghshire/Kirkcusbrightshire, Scotland.[37] [38] Their first four children were born in Abercorn. Barbara Nimmo, the last of their children to be born in Abercorn, was born in 1839.

---

[32] "Scotland, Marriages, 1561-1910," index. *FamilySearch.org* database entry for Matthew Nimmo, 1795.

[33] "Scotland, Select Births and Baptisms, 1564-1950." *Ancestry.com* database entry for Matthew Nimmo, spouse: Janet Davie.

[34] Hunter, Barbara L. "Matthew Nimmo - Hunter Wright Engelhardt Feldtman." (Ancestry Family Tree) Owner: hunterbl175. *Ancestry.com* database.

[35] "1841, 1851, 1861, Scotland Census." *Ancestry.com* database entry for David Nimmo.

[36] "Miriam Webster." *Google* database entry for "joiner." (19 Jan 2016)

[37] "Household transcription, 1851 Census." *findmypast.co.uk* database entry for Thomas Nimmo, b. 1845.

[38] 1861, Scotland Census." *Ancestry.com* database entry for Jane Nimms (Jane Nimmo).

The remaining 4 children were born in Kirkliston, Linlithgow, Scotland - including **Thomas Nimmo**, George's father, who was born on December 18, 1844 in Kirkliston.[39] [40]

Considering that David and Jane's first 4 children were born in Abercorn and that their last 4 were born in Kirkliston, it appears that the David Nimmo family moved to Kirkliston in about 1840.

Kirkliston (pronounced K'liston) is a parish about 9 miles south-west of Edinburgh, Scotland. Part of the parish is in the County of Edinburgh. The other part is in the County of Linlithgow. Within the parish are the villages of Kirkliston, Newbridge, Niddry and Nichburg.[41]

Children of David Nimmo (1803) and Jane/Jean McGill (1808)[42]

1.	Jessie	1830
2.	Mary	1831
3.	Agnes	1834
4.	Barbara	1839
5.	David	1842
6.	**Thomas**	1844
7.	Jane	1847
8.	Hugh	1851
9.	Margaret	1852

Thomas Nimmo. In the 1851 Scotland Census, Thomas Nimmo, George Nimmo's father, was listed as a "scholar."[43] By the 1861 census, Thomas, now in his teens, was listed as an "apprentice engineer," an occupation which might, at that time, have included skills used by a builder or a

---

[39] "1841 Scotland Census." *Ancestry.com* database entry for David Nimmo.

[40] "Household transcription, 1851 Census." *findmypast.co.uk* database entry for Thomas Nimmo, b. 1845.

[41] To complicate matters of geography, the Parish of Kirkliston is also in the Presbytery of Linlithgow. "National Gazetteer." www.genuki.org.uk database entry for Kirkliston. (4 Nov 1012)

[42] Hunter, Barbara L. "David Nimmo - Hunter Wright Engelhardt Feldtman." (Ancestry Family Tree) Owner: hunterbl175. *Ancestry.com* database.

[43] "household transcription, 1851 census." *findpast.co.uk* database entry for Thomas Nimmo.

contractor.[44]

On June 2, 1865, Thomas Nimmo, now 20 years old, married **Marion Kerr Chalmers** in Kirkliston, West Lothian, Scotland.[45] Marion Chalmers, who was born in Kirkliston on October 22, 1845, would have been 19 at the time of her marriage.[46]

The Marion Kerr Chalmers' Family. Marion Kerr Chalmers's father, George Chalmers, was born in Carde (Currie), Midlothian, Scotland on October 31, 1813.[47] Her mother, Mary Kerr, was born on Oct 3, 1814 in Kirkliston, Linlithgow.[48] Although George and Mary Chalmers's first child was born in Corstorphine, Midlothian, Scotland,[49] the Chalmers apparently moved to Kirkliston in about 1839[50] because the rest of their children were born there - including **Marion Kerr Chalmers**, George Nimmo's mother.[51] She was born in Kirkliston on October 22, 1845.[52]

---

[44] "household transcription, 1861 census." *findmypast.co.uk* database entry for Thomas Nimmo.

[45] "Scotland, Marriage's, 1561-1910, Thomas Nimmo, 1865." *FamilySearch.org* database entry for Thomas Nimmo.

[46] "Scotland, Births and Baptisms, 1564-1950, Marion Kerr Chalmers, 1845." *FamilySearch.org* database entry for Marion Kerr Chalmers. (7 Nov 2012)

[47] "Scotland, Select Births and Baptisms, 1564-1950." *Ancestry.com* database entry for George Chalmers.

[48] "Scotland, Births, and Baptisms, 1564-1950." *Ancestry.com* database entry for Mary Kerr.

[49] "1851, 1861, 1901, Scotland Census" Ancestry.com database entry for Margaret Chalmers.

[50] The Chalmers Family apparently arrived in Kirkliston about the same time as the Nimmos – that is, sometime in 1839 or 1840.

[51] "Scotland, Births, and Baptisms, 1564-1950." *Ancestry.com* database entry for George Chalmers (father) and Mary Kerr (mother).

[52] "Scotland, Births, and Baptisms, 1564-1950. *FamilySearch.org* database entry for Marion Kerr Chalmers.

Children of George Chalmers (1813) and Mary Kerr (1814)[53]

1.	Margaret	1837	Corstorphine, Scotland
2.	Agnes	1839	Kirkliston, Scotland
3.	Alexander	1843	Kirkliston, Scotland
4.	**Marion Kerr**	1845	Kirkliston, Scotland
5.	Janet Jemima	1848	Kirkliston, Scotland
6.	John	1850	Kirkliston, Scotland
7.	George	1854	Kirkliston, Scotland

Thomas Nimmo and Marion Kerr Chalmers. Thomas and Marion Nimmo, George Nimmo's parents, had their first child, David Chalmers Nimmo, on July 13, 1865 in Kirkliston.[54] David appears to be named after his grandfather, David Nimmo. Given the date of the Nimmo's marriage, June 2, 1865, and the date of the birth of their first child, I suspect that Marion Chalmers Nimmo had some real concern as to whether they would "make it to the church on time."

Their second child, **George Nimmo**, was born in Kirkliston, Scotland on February 13, 1867.[55] George seems to be named after his mother's father, George Chalmers. George Nimmo was **Rose** Nimmo's father.

---

[53] Hunter, Barbara L. "George Chalmers - Hunter Wright Engelhardt Feldtman." (Ancestry Family Tree) Owner: hunterbl175. *Ancestry.com* database.

[54] "Scotland, Births and Baptisms, 1564-1950, Thomas Nimmo in entry for Davie Nimmo, 1865" *FamilySearch.org* database entry for Thomas Nimmo.

[55] "Scotland, Births and Baptisms, 1564-1950, Thomas Nimmo in entry for George Nimmo, 1867." *FamilySearch.org* database entry for George Nimmo.

3
EMIGRATION
COURAGE AND DETERMINATION

In late March of 1868, just a year after the British North American colonies formed the Dominion of Canada and about three years after the American Civil War ended, Thomas Nimmo, his wife, Marion, and his two very young sons, David and George, boarded the transatlantic steamship, S/S Britannia, in Glasgow, Scotland to begin their long journey to Ontario, Canada.

The Britannia was a Scottish "emigrant ship,"[56] owned and operated by the Anchor Line, which made voyages between Glasgow, Scotland and New York City in the United States.[57] The ship was less than 262 feet in length. That is, it was 87 yards long – somewhat less than an American football field. And, it was just over 33 feet across the beam- just little better than the yards needed for a first down. Therefore, the Britannia was a long, narrow ship - about 8 times as long as it was wide. It looked like a modified clipper ship - made of iron. It had 3 masts and a long, sweeping prow to

---

[56] I seem to have created confusion with my use of both "emigrant" and "immigrant." An "emigrant" leaves a country. The Nimmos emigrated from Scotland. An "immigrant" goes to another country so the Nimmos immigrated to Canada.

[57] "Anchor Line (steamship company)." *Wikipedia*. https://en.wikipedia.org/wiki/Anchor_Line_(steamship_company). (Accessed: 3 Sep 2017)

accommodate sails – in case its steam engine failed. However, the Britannia was primarily a steamship so it had a funnel at mid-ships and a single screw which allowed the ship to cross the Atlantic at a speed of 10 knots per hour.[58] [59]

An advertisement for Anchor Line of Transatlantic Steamships in the 1869 Saint John Daily Evening News proclaimed one could book a cabin for 13 guineas and that steamship ticket in steerage could be had for less than ½ that amount- just 6 guineas.[60] That meant the Nimmo family could have paid about 24 guineas[61] for their passage to New York, although the children, David and George, might have cost somewhat less. Never-the-less, the Nimmo's must have made a determined effort to save for the voyage as it is estimated that it might have taken about 1/3 of a working man's yearly income to pay the cost of a family's emigration.[62]

Like many emigrant families,[63] the Nimmos would probably had said their goodbyes to their families back home in Kirkliston and then have boarded the train for the 50-mile trip to Glasgow - all the time knowing that, unless some members of their family emigrated to the United States or Canada, this would be the last time they would ever see their family.

---

[58] "Norway-Heritage, Hands Across the Sea. SS Britannia (1), Anchor Line." http://www.norwayheritage.com/p_ship.asp?sh=brit0. (Accessed: 11 Nov 2017)

[59] Ayre, Elaine Melby. *The Princess Doll's Scrapbook*. Victoria, Canada: Friesen Press, 2014. Pp. 73.

[60] "Anchor Line." (advertisement) *Saint John's Evening News*, August 2, 1969, page 2. *Google News Archive Search*. Database. (Accessed: 9 Nov 2017)

[61] It's difficult to translate old currency into today's dollars. But under the old system of British currency, a guinea was worth one pound and 1 shilling.

[62] Huber, Leslie Albrecht. "Understanding Your Immigrant Ancestors: Voyage to the U.S." *Understanding Your Immigrant Ancestors.com*. 2006, 2007, 2008. http://www.understandingyourancestors.com/ia/shipvoyage.aspx. (Accessed: 10 Nov 2017)

[63] Ibid. Huber.

Once at the Anchor Steamship Lines in Glasgow, the Nimmos still had many things to do, including passing their health examinations. The discovery of a family member with a contagious disease could keep the family on the Glasgow docks for months.[64]

In late March of 1868, 322 passengers boarded the S/S Britannia. Five passengers had cabins. The rest, 317 passengers, were making the voyage in steerage.

Even today you can find the Nimmo's names on the Britannia's 1868 passenger list:[65]

Passenger List **Anchor Line of Transatlantic Steam Packet Ships**[66]
𝔇istrict of 𝔑ew 𝔜ork – 𝔓ort of 𝔑ew 𝔜ork

65	. . . .				
66	. . . .				
67 Thomas Nimmo	23 yrs. Engineer	Scotland	United States	steerage	
68 Marion	22 yrs.	"	"	"	
69 David	2 yrs.	"	"	"	
70 George	10 mo.	"	"	"	

It is easy to picture[67] the Thomas Nimmo family on that momentous March day in 1868 - bundled in layers of clothing - trudging determinedly up the gangplank to the S/S Britannia's main deck from the Glasgow docks.[68] Thomas, 23 years old, might have been carrying everything they

---

[64] Ibid. Huber.

[65] "New York, Passenger Lists, 1820-1957, 1868, Arrival: New York, New York." *Ancestry.com* database entry for Thomas Nimmo.

[66] "New York, Passenger Lists, 1820-1957, 1868, Arrival: New York, New York." *Ancestry.com* database entry for Thomas Nimmo.

[67] I am imagining this – but, from my reading and from internet images of "immigrant ship life," I think I've captured, with some accuracy, the spirit and the difficulty of the transatlantic voyage for the Nimmos.

[68] The Britannia was only about 21 feet in height, and even less of the ship could be seen above water level, so one should not picture a tall ship (unless you include the masts) or a very long trudge up a gangplank. Height of ship is given in: "Norway-Heritage, Hands Across the Sea."

needed during their 14 day voyage to New York: clothes, extra food, containers for the daily allotment of water, utensils, bedding and other precious belongings.[69] Marion might have been grasping the hand of her two year old son, David, while holding tightly to the 10 month old baby, George.

Once on board, the four Nimmos along with 313 other passengers were crowded into "steerage" for the duration of the voyage.[70] [71] That meant that all 317 steerage passengers would have been packed into single, large room-like area, just below the main deck - a room that originally was meant for cargo and some of the ship's steering equipment. This cargo hold, usually about 6-8 feet high, was reached by steep stairs (and no railing) from the main deck.

Typically, narrow trestle tables were arranged, end-to-end, down the middle of the room - with detached benches on either side of the tables. Bunks, intended to accommodate 5-6 people each, were attached to the walls on each side of the "room."

It is likely that the four Nimmos shared a single bunk. If they were lucky there would have been enough room for family members to sit up without bumping their head. Their belongings, which they had carried aboard, would have been lashed to their bunk with ropes.

There were no partitions. No Privacy. Generally, the single ladies had bunks in the bow, the families occupied bunks in the middle portion of the ship, and single men took bunks in the stern.[72] Obviously, the Nimmos, passenger numbers 67, 68, 69 and 70, traveled as a family and were able to

---

http://www.norwayheritage.com/p_ship.asp?sh=brit0. (Accessed: 11 Nov 2017)

[69] Given the space restrictions aboard ship, the Nimmos, would only have been able to bring the bare essentials when they emigrated.

[70] Google images of "immigrant ships" will show you amazing pictures of life in the ship's steerage.

[71] "Norway-Heritage, Hands Across the Sea."
http://www.norwayheritage.com/steerage.htm. (Accessed: 11 Nov 2017)

[72] Ayre, Elaine Melby. *The Princess Doll's Scrapbook*. Victoria, Canada: Friesen Press, 2014. Pp. 79. I have also been told that it was just the opposite. That is, the single women were in the stern and the single men were bunking in the bow where the passage would have been rougher.

occupy a more desirable space in the middle of the ship where the passengers would be least affected by the ship's roll and plunge during a storm.

All the passengers must have crowded to the rails as the S/S Britannia sailed down the River Clyde, into the Firth of Clyde and then past Scotland's outer islands. For many of those emigrants, including the Nimmos, it would be the last time they would ever see Scotland.

It took Britannia about 14 days to travel over 3,000 miles from Glasgow to New York. Certainly, fourteen days in steerage, packed with 317 people, made for a difficult trip. Steerage was dim as well as cramped. Fires - either for light, warmth or cooking - were not allowed on board ship. As one can imagine, sanitation and ventilation were also a problem.

In bad weather, the hatches were battened down which made the lighting, ventilation and sanitation situation so much worse. In addition to the generally deteriorating living conditions during bad weather, including seasickness from the pitching and rolling of the ship, Atlantic storms also were a source of real danger. For the Anchor Steamship Line alone, in its 50 years of operation, 20 ships were lost at sea.[73] One of these ships was the S/S Britannia, which, after just 10 years of operation, was wrecked on the Isle of Arran, Scotland in 1873.[74]

But, all of these difficulties were not unexpected, and steamship travel was a vast improvement over early emigrant experiences on sailing ships. Those early emigrants would have spent about 3 times as long in steerage before they reached New York, and they would have had to provide their own food - which could run out if the voyage took longer than expected.

By the time the Nimmos sailed, laws required that the steerage passengers be provided meals. Steerage passengers in 1868 would have been provided some basic food. Perhaps, it would have been soups or stews of peas, beans, rice, boiled potatoes, vegetables and some sort of preserved meat such as salt pork. Also, bread, salt, tea, molasses and a daily ration of water would have been provided.[75] [76] Though meals were not elegant by any

---

[73] "Norway-Heritage, Hands Across the Sea."
http://www.norwayheritage.com/p_ship.asp?sh=brit0. (Accessed: 11 Nov 2017)

[74] "Anchor Line (steamship company)." *Wikipedia*.
https://en.wikipedia.org/wiki/Anchor_Line_(steamship_company). (Accessed: 3 Sep 2017)

[75] Bernardin. "The Foods That Passed Through Ellis Island| Arts & Culture."
(January 6, 2010) www.smithsonianmag.com/arts.../the-foods-that-passed-

means, at least passengers on the SS Britannia would not have to worry about running out of food.

Although there must have been some conflicts[77] as the emigrants jostled for space and resources, it is also possible the passengers in steerage were compatible and supportive. Most of the adult passengers in Britannia's steerage were working class people in their teens or twenties. There were very few passengers over that age. These steerage passengers gave their occupations as: joiners, farmers, servants, bakers, teachers, miners, gardeners, watchmen, carpenters, coachmen, and - like Thomas Nimmo did - engineers. Most were from Ireland and Scotland. Except for a lone German in Britannia's steerage who was ship's passenger number one, a few Englishmen made up the remainder of the steerage passengers.[78] All these working people had saved long and hard for a voyage to a better life. It is easy to imagine that the steerage passengers had lively, interesting conversations about their plans, hopes and dreams during their voyage.

The S/S Britannia arrived at Castle Garden in New York Harbor on the 7th of April 1868.[79] Castle Garden, a converted fort on the lower Manhattan waterfront, was a place, in 1868, where US government registered the immigrants and also provided much of the needed safety and many of the basic services immigrants needed.

Besides being able to safely exchange money, get travel information, and buy train tickets, the Nimmos would have been able to sleep on the floor of the Castle Garden facility for a couple of days while they rested for the next leg of their journey.[80]

---

through-ellis-island-76907163/ https://www.smithsonianmag.com/arts-culture/the-foods-that-passed-through-ellis-island-76907163/. (Accessed: 12 Nov 2017)

[76] "Table 1. – Food supply per passenger required on ships bound to the United States ports from the ports indicated, 1854." U. S. Government publication.

[77] To keep conflict to a minimum, the captain enforced strict rules for the emigrant passengers.

[78] "New York, Passenger Lists, 1820-1957, 1868, Arrival: New York, New York." *Ancestry.com* database entry for Thomas Nimmo.

[79] "New York, Passenger Lists, 1820-1957, 1868, Arrival: New York, New York." *Ancestry.com* database entry for Thomas Nimmo.

[80] Huber, Leslie Albrecht. "Understanding Your Ancestors: Immigrant Ancestors:

***

The Nimmos still had about 550 miles and many, many days to travel, possibly by both train and steamship,[81] to reach their final destination - Ontario, Canada.[82]

Voyage to the U.S.: The Entryway at Castle Garden."
http://www.understandingyourancestors.com/ia/entrywayAtCastleGrden.aspx.
(Accessed" 10 Nov 2017)

[81] "The family may have taken the train all the way from NYC through to Ontario, or they may have crossed Lake Ontario by ship. If they first arrived in Elgin County, they likely took the train from Niagara through to their destination." Email from Elysia DeLaurentis, Archives Assistant, Wellington County Museum and Archives, 0536 Wellington Road 18, Fergus, ON N1M 2W3 Canada, www.wellington.ca/museum.

[82] It is just speculation that the Nimmos were initially headed to Ontario ---and Elgin county in particular. But that scenario seems the most reasonable given the circumstances described in this book.

BARBARA L. HUNTER

4

ONTARIO, CANADA

The Nimmos were part of the great immigration of European settlers to the Canadian countryside who, along with the original Canadian pioneers, helped build the country of Canada.[83]

The Canadian Census of 1871, enumerated about 3 years after the Nimmos immigrated to Canada, shows that the Nimmos were living in the Southwold Township of Elgin County in the province of Ontario, Canada. The family now included two more children, Thomas and Mary, who had been born after the family settled in Ontario.

At the time of the 1871 census, May 4th, 1871, the Nimmo's third son, Thomas, was almost 2 years old.[84] Their first daughter, Mary, was just a

---

[83] It is likely that for most of their 2 ½ years of marriage, and probably even before that, the Nimmos planned to emigrate. It simply would have taken that long to acquire the money and resources for the entire family to move abroad. Therefore, it seems that the Nimmos always had the pioneering spirit. Cost of voyage in Huber, Leslie Albrecht. "Understanding Your Ancestors: Immigrant Ancestors: Voyage to the U.S.: The Entryway at Castle Garden." http://www.understandingyourancestors.com/ia/shipsvoyaghe.aspx. (Accessed: 10 Nov 2017)

[84] Although the 1871 Canadian Census shows Thomas Nimmo as being 1 year of age, Thomas was actually almost 2 years old at the time of the census. He was born in May of 1869 and the census –for the portion in which the Nimmos were accounted for- was enumerated on the 4th of May 1871.

month old. David, the oldest child, at 5 years of age, was attending school. George, who was only 4, was at home with his younger brother and sister.[85]

Southwold Township, where the Nimmos lived, is not a town; it is a political sub-district of Elgin County. The townships of Elgin County, Ontario, are spread out like an arch along part of Lake Erie's northern shore. Close to the middle, looking like a wedged-shaped cap stone, is Southwold Township.[86]

Southwold Township is a bit over 100 square miles - about 10 miles across from border to border. From the top of a tall barn, you might see for miles - over virtually flat farmland. Generally, the view would be broken only by modest farm houses and clumps of deciduous trees that would be scattered here and there.[87]

In 1871, if you looked hard enough over Southwold Township, you might see a cluster of homes and businesses about 5 miles from the northern shore of Lake Erie – just about 7 miles north and west of Port Stanley. This would be the "Village" of Fingal, where the Nimmos were living.[88] [89] [90] At the time there were about 500 people living in Fingal.[91]

---

[85] "1871, Census of Canada, Southwold, Elgin West, Ontario." *Ancestry.com* database entry for Thomas Nimmo.

[86] "Southwold, Ontario." *Wikipedia.* https://en.wikipedia.org/wiki/Southwold_Ontario. (Accessed: 18 Nov 2017) and "Elgin County." Wikipedia. https://en.wikipedia.org/wiki/Elgin_County. (Accessed: 18 Nov 2017)

[87] Any "street view" on Google Maps will confirm this impression. *Google Maps* database entry for Southwold, Elgin County, Ontario. https://www.google.com/maps/place/Southwold. (Accessed: 21 Nov 2017)

[88] "Assessment Roll for the Township of Southwold, 1870, 1871, 1872." Copies supplied by Gena Dewaele, Elgin County Archives.

[89] No other records of the Nimmos in Fingal have been found at this time, so perhaps they moved on after 1872. Gena Dewaele, Elgin County Archives: email to Barbara Hunter. (1 Mar 2018)

[90] "Fingal, Ontario." *Google Maps* database entry for Fingal, Ontario. https://www.google.com/maps/place/Fingal. (Accessed: 1 Mar 2018)

[91] A small excerpt from the "Elgin Times OGST Web Page Three." Forwarded to me by Pat Adam of the Oxford Branch of the Ontario Genealogical Society.

The Nimmo's neighbors were mostly families whose "origins" were "Scotland," "Ireland," and "England."[92] A very few families were of German origin and even fewer were French. Many of the older people were immigrants, like the Nimmos, but many of the children in these large families had been born in Ontario.[93]

There was a mixture of religions represented in the population of Southwold township. Generally, it seems that those families of Irish origin were Roman Catholic, the Scots were Presbyterian,[94] and the English were Church of England, Methodist or Baptists. But, of course, not everyone fit this pattern. There was even one "Free Thinker."[95]

Since Southwold was rich agricultural land, the Nimmos were surrounded by many "farmers," and "laborers." However, the 1871 Canadian Census shows that Thomas Nimmo was a "machinist" and that his nearest neighbors were machinists, "moulders," and shoemakers. Other close neighbors were coopers, a butcher, blacksmiths, two "merchants," a rake maker, and a "speculator." The 18-year-old daughter of one of the Scottish Presbyterian families was the "school mistress." Her 22-year-old sister, also living at home, was a "milliner."[96]

Thomas Nimmo might have worked at any one of the business in Fingal: the tannery, the saw mill, the shoemakers, a blacksmith or even the cheese factory. However, it is most likely that Thomas Nimmo, a machinist, worked for Macpherson, Glasgow and Company, a highly successful foundry located in Fingal.[97] [98]

---

[92] "Origins" on the 1871 Census of Canada meant "European Origins." Although there were several members of families that came to Canada from the United States, these individuals still had to state their European "Origin."

[93] "1871; Census of Canada, Southwold, Elgin West, Ontario." *Ancestry.com* database entry for Thomas Nimmo.

[94] The Nimmos always listed themselves as Presbyterian.

[95] "1871; Census of Canada, Southwold, Elgin West, Ontario." *Ancestry.com* database entry for Thomas Nimmo.

[96] "1871; Census of Canada, Southwold, Elgin West, Ontario." *Ancestry.com* database entry for Thomas Nimmo.

[97] In about 1872, Fingal had a cheese factory, a marble works, a cabinet works, a tannery, a flour and lumber mill, a saw mill and veneer factory as well as 3 hotels. It also had a foundry which manufactured farm equipment. In: a small

In 1848, Daniel Macpherson, himself a Scots immigrant, along with William Glasgow and Matthias Hovey, started with a small shop and foundry in Fingal. By the time Thomas Nimmo reached Fingal, Macpherson, Glasgow and Company was a sophisticated operation that produced farm equipment such as grain crushers, plows, cultivators and threshing machines.[99]

Since the owner of the foundry and most of the "machinists" were Scots Presbyterians, Thomas Nimmos would have found a comfortably familiar working situation in Fingal, Southwold, Ontario.

But, as none of the Scots in the immediate area seem to have emigrated at the same time as the Nimmos, it is possible that the Nimmo's first knowledge and connection with the Fingal community and the foundry was not through a friend or relative in Ontario, but through their Scots Presbyterian Church, newspaper articles or their neighbors back in Kirkliston, Scotland.

***

While Thomas and Marion Nimmo were establishing themselves in Southwold, Ontario, three of Marion Nimmo's sisters immigrated to the Detroit, Michigan area of the United States.[100]

Mary Chalmers came to Detroit in about 1870 and married Alfred Bates on December 14, 1870.[101]

Then, in 1871, Agnes Chalmers McVittie emigrated with her husband,

---

excerpt from the "Elgin Times OGST Web Page Three." Forwarded to me by Pat Adam of the Oxford Branch of the Ontario Genealogical Society.

[98] Excellent suggestion and information on Macpherson, Glasgow and Company provided by Pat Adam of the Oxford Branch of the Ontario Genealogical Society.

[99] Turner, H. S. "Canadian Notes – the Macpherson Machinery." *The Farm Collector.* May 1952. https://www/farmcollector.com/steam-tractiio/canadian- notes-may-1952. (Accessed: 1 Mar 2018)

[100] Detroit is only about 130 miles from Southwold, Ontario.

[101] Mary Chalmers, an older sister of Marion Nimmo, may even have been the first one in her family to emigrate - perhaps as early as 1865. But it is more likely she emigrated around 1870 and, shortly thereafter, married her husband, Alfred Bates, on the 14th of December, 1870, in Detroit. In: "Michigan, Marriage Records, 1867-1952." *Ancestry.com* database entry for Mary Chalmers.

John McVittie, a miller. They brought their 3 children with them: Margaret, 4, Mary, 2, and William, 10 months.[102]

Finally, in 1872, Janet Jemima Chalmers Pringle immigrated to Detroit with her husband, John Pringle, and their son, Robert.[103] [104] They also settled in Michigan where they had two more children, George and John.[105] All the rest of the Chalmers and Nimmos seem to have stayed in Scotland.[106]

By 1880 things had changed for the Nimmo, Bates and Pringle families. Mary Chalmers Bates and her husband, Alfred, were in San Francisco, California with 3 children. One of their children had been born in Detroit, William Edwin Bates in 1872. By 1880, they had had two more children in San Francisco: Charles Henry Bates in 1878 and Lilly M. Bates in 1880.[107] [108]

By 1880, John and Janet Jemma Chalmers Pringle were living in Oakland California. Their home was just across the San Francisco Bay from

---

[102] "New York, Passenger Lists, 1820-1957. 1871, Arrival: New York, New York." *Ancestry.com* database entry for John McVittie.

[103] They had an older daughter, Mary, but she did not emigrate with them and does not appear in later records so I suspect she died when she was very young.

[104] "1880, United States Federal Census." (Oakland, Alameda, California) *Ancestry.com* database entry for Jemima Pringle.

[105] "1880, United States Federal Census." (Oakland, Alameda, California). *Ancestry.com* database entry for Jemima Pringle.

[106] Marion Kerr Chalmers Nimmo's oldest sister, Margaret married George Forest and stayed in Scotland, perhaps to help her family, as her mother, who without the presence of her husband, seems, by 1861, to have fallen on hard times. In the 1861 Scotland Census, Mary Kerr Chalmers' occupation was listed as "Field Worker Pauper." In: "1861 Scotland Census." *Ancestry.com* database entry for Mary Kerr Chalmers.

[107] "1880 United States Federal Census." (San Francisco, San Francisco, California). *Ancestry.com* database entry for Mary Bates.

[108] "Died. Bates, Lilly M." *The San Francisco Call*. 17 Nov 1897. Pg. 13. *Newspapers.com* database entry for Lilly Bates.

the Bates Family. The Pringles had added four more children to their family. George Pringle was born in Detroit in 1872. Three years later, in 1875, John Pringle was born - also in Detroit. Two Pringle daughters were born in Oakland: Minnie in 1877 and Matilda Ann (Tilly) in 1880.[109] Then, at the age of 32, Marion Nimmo's sister, Janet Jemima Chalmers Pringle died on December 20, 1880.[110]

***

By 1878, the Nimmos had also moved on. However, they did not join the Bates, Pringle or McVittie families in the United States, but instead, the Nimmos moved further north to the Village of Mount Forest, Wellington, Ontario.[111] [112]

Mount Forest is almost 120 miles north of Fingal. Although Fingal, Mount Forest, and the areas around them were formed by the same repeated glaciation which eventually produced the vast, flat areas of highly productive farmland of southern Ontario, Mount Forest is at a much higher elevation than Fingal. At an elevation of about 1400 feet, with moist, cold air sweeping up from the Great Lakes, Mount Forest is in the "snow belt" which means that the Mount Forest area can have up to 100 inches of snowfall a year. The frosty period starts in late September and doesn't end until late May. From the middle of November to the end of March, it is generally below freezing.[113] The difficulty of enduring a winter of bitter

---

[109] "1880, United States Federal Census." (San Francisco, San Francisco, California) *Ancestry.com* database entry for John Pringle. (Note: Matilda Ann's (Tilly's) birthday is generally interpreted as October or November 1879. A closer look at the original 1880 U. S. Census indicates her birthday should be March of 1880.)

[110] "Obituary." (newspaper notice) *Oakland Tribune* - 21 Dec 1880 - Page 4. *Newspapers.com* database entry for Jemima Pringle.

[111] "1878, Assessment, Roll for the Village of Mount Forest." Thomas Nimmo, Machinist, was renting from Thomas Watt. Provided by Elysia DeLaurentis, Wellington County Museums and Archives.

[112] Originally, Mount Forest straddled the line between two Ontario counties, Wellington and Grey- with both county councils trying to annex this thriving area.

[113] *Portrait – A History of the Arthur Area.* Compiled by Paul O'Donnell and Frank D. Coffey. Municipality of Arthur, Ontario, 1971.

weather is the only thing that comes to mind when thinking of the Nimmos in this environment.

Winters aside, Mount Forest occupied the higher land near the head-waters of the Saugeen River - which made it an ideal place to build mills and factories that relied on water power.

In 1853, just 25 years before the Nimmos moved to Mount Forest., the first lots were surveyed by Francis Kerr.[114] In the 25-year period, from when the land was surveyed until the Nimmos arrived at Mount Forest, the Mount Forest area had been transformed. In the 1850's and 1860's, mills and factories sprung up: a grist mill, a flour mill, an axe factory (which also produced "edge tools"), a steam mill which produced lumber, a chair and furniture factory, a tannery, two foundries, a carriage factory, a potash factory which also produced soap and candles, and, of course, a brewery.[115]

A gravel turnpike road was built in 1861.[116] It would take a teamster one day to drive his team the 40 miles from Mount Forest to Guelph (Guelf was further south near Lake Erie) with produce from Mount Forest. It would take another day to drive back with merchandise for a store in Mount Forest.[117] That is- it took that long when the roads were passable.

By 1864, the population had grown to 1153 so that Mount Forest qualified to be incorporated as a village.[118]

By 1871, Mount Forest had 10 hotels, eight churches, and 18 stores. (It also had a newspaper and schools.)[119] On December 16th of that year, the Grey and Bruce Railway, its cars pulled by a wood-burning engine, began service to Mount Forest. The railroad connected Mount Forest to ports on Lake Erie and Lake Huron and to all the goods and services provided in the City of Toronto. Having regular rail service spurred more growth in the

---

[114] "Mount Forest, Ontario." *Wikipedia.* http//en.wikipedia.org/wiki/Mount_Forest,_Ontario. Database entry for Mount Forest, Ontario. (Accessed: 6 Jun 2013)

[115] "Directory of the County of Grey, (Ontario) for 1865-1866." Freepages.genealogy.rootsweb.ancestry.com/wjmartin/grey5.htm.

[116] *Historical Atlas of Wellington County*-Town of Mount Forest. 1903. Pp. 8, 9.

[117] Edwards, William J. *Mount Forest – The Way We Were.* Boston: The Boston Mills Press, 1979. Pp. 47.

[118] "Mount Forest, Ontario." *Wikipedia.* (Accessed: 6 Nov 2012)

[119] "Mount Forest, Ontario." *Wikipedia.* (Accessed: 6 Nov 2012)

Village of Mount Forest.[120] By 1875, the population was around 1700 people.[121]

When the Nimmos arrived in 1878, Mount Forest was a thriving center of commerce with enhanced opportunities for schooling, entertainment, and jobs. It was a commercial center that primarily served the needs of the farmers of the surrounding area. It had several hotels, 2 newspapers, schools, churches serving various denominations, many manufacturing establishments, a bank, an assembly hall, and an abundance of stores and other businesses.

All this might have been very attractive to the Nimmos with their growing family, but it was probably the specific opportunity of a job for Thomas Nimmo at the Vulcan Forge that brought them north to Mount Forest.

In 1877, H. H. Soval, one of the Soval brothers who published "The Mount Forest Confederate,"[122] a well-respected local newspaper, decided to refit and restart the Vulcan Foundry which had been inactive for about 7 years.[123] Once the Vulcan Forge was up and running, Vulcan Forge produced a wide variety of goods and services. You could get all sorts of engine, boiler and machine work, casting, pipe fitting, forging and general blacksmithing at the Vulcan Forge. The forge made metal (brass and iron) products – everything from bolts to larger castings of every description - including cast iron columns for buildings.[124] Evidently, if you could cast it or if you could machine it on a metal lathe, the Vulcan Forge could produce

---

[120] Edwards, William J. *Mount Forest – The Way We Were*. Boston: The Boston Mills Press, 1979. Pp. 47, 48.

[121] "Fisher & Taylor's Gazetteer and General Directory of the County of Wellington 1875-76." Toronto: Fisher & Taylor, Publishers: 1876. Pp. 198.

[122] "The "Confederate" is a reference to the Confederation that formed the Dominion of Canada. - not the Confederate soldiers of the American Civil War.

[123] "Resurrected." (newspaper article) *The Mount Forest Confederate*. September 4, 1877. Pp. 2.

[124] In 1867, the Vulcan Foundry was a major manufacturer of large items such as printing presses, steam engines, threshing machines, stoves and drag saws. In: Edwards, William J. *Mount Forest – The Way We Were*. Boston: The Boston Mills Press, 1979. Pp. 74.

it for its customers.[125] The Vulcan Forge, or the Vulcan Iron Works as it was also called, could and did use the expert machinist skills of Thomas Nimmo.[126]

By 1878 the Nimmos were renting a home on Elgin Street, just one block off of Main Street which was the local shopping area for Mount Forest.[127] The next year, 1879, the Nimmos were renting on Normanby Street.[128] Normanby Street, in Mount Forest, was where the Nimmo's daughter, Jane (Jean) Nimmo was born on July 6, 1879.[129] [130]

Then, in 1880 and 1881, the Nimmos rented a home near the west side of Main Street. In the 1881 Canadian Census, Thomas Nimmo was 35 and Marion was one year younger. David, 15, and George, 13, were teenagers. Both were in school. Thomas, 11, and Mary, 9, were also in school. Jane, at 2, was at home.[131]

---

[125] "The Vulcan Iron Works.," (Advertisement) *Mount Forest Confederate*, 14 Dec 1882. Pp. 3.

[126] "Hand Hurt." (newspaper article) *Mount Forest Confederate*, 14 Dec 1882. Pp. 4.

[127] "1878, Mount Forest Tax Assessment Roll. Nos 327." For Thomas Watt, owner. Provided by: Elysia DeLaurentis, Wellington County Museum and Archives.

[128] "1879, Mount Forest Tax Assessment Roll. Nos. 354 and 355." For John Morrison, owner. Provided by: Elysia DeLaurentis, Wellington County Museum and Archives.

[129] "Ontario Birth Registration, Mount Forest, Wellington, 1879." For Jane Nimmo. Provided by: Elysia DeLaurentis, Wellington County Museum and Archives.

[130] There is an 8-year gap in the ages of the Nimmo children. Their oldest daughter, Mary, was born in 1871. Their next child that we know about was Jane (Jean D.) Nimmo, born in Mount Forest, Wellington, Ontario on July 6, 1879. Since Marion Nimmo, on the 1900 United Census, had 11 children, 7 of who were living, it is possible that Marion and Thomas Nimmo had 3 children in the 8-year period between 1871 and 1879 - and lost all 3 of them.

[131] "1881, Census of Canada. Mount Forest, Wellington North, Ontario." *Ancestry.com* database entry for Thomas Nimmo.

Just as in Fingal, the Nimmo's Mount Forest neighbors were still primarily of Scots, Irish or English origins (even if some of those people did emigrate from the United States). Thomas Nimmo was still listed as a "machinist." The Nimmo neighbors now included brick layers, store clerks, merchants, cabinet makers, dress makers, carriage makers, "Drep makers," stone masons and finishers, an "osler," agents, bookkeepers, hotel keepers, a postmaster, someone who worked in the "telegraph office," agents, blacksmiths, tailors, teachers – including a "high school teacher" and a "music teacher," - and several "gentlemen."[132]

The Nimmo's next child, Alexander Hughey Nimmo, was born in Arthur, North Wellington, Canada on May 16, 1882.[133] Arthur, Wellington, Canada is not very far from Mount Forest so perhaps the Nimmos had briefly moved a short way from Mount Forest to the Village of Arthur.[134]

On Saturday, December 9th, 1882, Thomas Nimmo was injured while working on a lathe at the Vulcan Foundry. A piece of metal "flew out" and hit the back of his hand. The cut required 3 stitches.[135] The very next day, less than seven months after Alexander's birth, Marion Chalmers Nimmo, was born in Mount Forest, Wellington, Canada.[136] Obviously, little Marion was a very premature baby. With a delicate baby and an injured breadwinner, December 1882 had to be a tough time for the Nimmos. The

---

[132] "1881, Census of Canada. Mount Forest, Wellington North, Ontario." *Ancestry.com* database entry for Thomas Nimmo.

[133] *The Book of Detroiters: a biographical dictionary of leading living men.* (1914) *AncestryInstitution.com* database entry for Alexander Nimmo.

[134] Alexander's recollection that he was born in Arthur and not Mount Forest could be an indication that the Nimmos briefly lived between Mount Forest and Arthur. However, I have found no registration of Alexander's birth in either location. The Nimmos were back in Mount Forest December of 1882 for the birth of Marion Chalmers Nimmo.

[135] "Hand Hurt." (newspaper article) *Mount Forest Confederate*, 14 Dec 1882. Pp. 4. Provided by Elysia DeLaurentis, Wellington County Museum and Archives.

[136] Marion was born on December 10, 1882. In: "Schedule A - Births." Wellington, Mount Forest. Marion (Father: Thomas Nimmo; Mother: Marion Chalmers). Provided by Elysia DeLaurentis, Wellington County Museum and Archives.

Nimmos were probably holding their breath because they didn't register Marion's birth until February of 1883.[137]

***

The Nimmos may have thought of building their own home in Mount Forest because, in 1884, Thomas Nimmo bought Lots 1 and 2 of Park Lot 6, just west of Normanby Street in Mount Forest.[138] However, there is no indication that the Nimmos ever built on the lots or lived there.[139] They continued to rent homes in Mount Forest within walking distance of Market Street through 1884.[140]

***

By 1885, the Nimmos were "non-residents of Mount Forest.[141] Maggie Nimmo was born on July 2, 1885 in Ingersoll, Oxford, Ontario,[142] which is south of Mount Forest – and much closer to Southwold Township.[143] David Nimmo, who listed himself as the "child's brother," registered

---

[137] "Schedule A - Births." Wellington, Mount Forest. Marion (Father: Thomas Nimmo; Mother: Marion Chalmers). Provided by Elysia DeLaurentis, Wellington County Museum and Archives.

[138] "Land Abstract Index, Mount Forest, Wellington County," Vol. 2. Pp. 33-34. Provided by: Elysia DeLaurentis, Wellington County Museum and Archives.

[139] In 1893, Thomas and Marion Nimmo, now nonresidents, sold their lots to Thomas Stoval. In: "Land Abstract Index, Mount Forest, Wellington County," Vol. 2. Pp. 33-34. Provided by Elysia DeLaurentis, Wellington County Museum and Archives.

[140] "1884, Mount Forest Tax Assessment Roll, West Ward." Provided by: Elysia DeLaurentis, Wellington County Museum and Archives.

[141] "1885, Mount Forest Tax Assessment Roll, West Ward." Provided by Elysia DeLaurentis, Wellington County Museum and Archives.

[142] "Ontario, Births and Baptisms, 1770-1899" *FamilySearch.org* database entry for Maggie Nimmo."

[143] There was the large Noxon Brothers Foundry in Ingersoll, but, except for David who says he is a resident, there is no record of the Nimmos living or working there. Suggestion and interesting information on Noxon Brothers Foundry provided by Pat Adam, Oxford Branch of the Ontario Genealogical society.

Maggie's birth July 6, 1885.[144] It does not appear that Maggie survived.[145]

***

Then, about 1885, after living 17 years in Ontario Canada, the Nimmos immigrated to the United States of America. Thomas was then 41 years old and Marion was 40.

Thomas and Marion Nimmo's Children in 1885[146]

Name	Born	Age in 1885
1. David	Kirkliston, Scotland (1865)	20
2. George[147]	**Kirkliston, Scotland (1867)**	**18**
3. Thomas Jr.	Elgin, Ontario, Canada (1869)	16
4. Mary	Elgin, Ontario, Canada (1871)	14
5. Jane/Jean	Mt. Forest, Wellington, Ontario (1879)	6
6. Alexander	Arthur, Wellington, Ontario (1882)	3
7. Marion Kerr	Mt. Forest, Wellington, Ontario (1882)	3
8. Maggie[148]	Ingersoll, Oxford, Canada (1885)	--

Thomas, Marion and most of their children settled in Detroit, Michigan. However, after a couple of years, David Nimmo returned to Canada.[149]

---

[144] This seems to indicate a possible pattern of Thomas Nimmo not registering the birth of his children who did not survive.

[145] The 1910 United States Federal Census states that Marion Kerr Chalmers Nimmo had 11 children, only 7 of which were living in 1910. As she is not found in other records, Maggie Nimmo must have been one of the four children that did not survive. In: "U. S. Census, 1910." (Detroit Ward 12, Wayne Michigan) *Ancestry.com* database entry for 'Marion Nimons' (Nimmo).

[146] Rose Nimmo's grandparents.

[147] Rose Nimmo's father.

[148] Maggie Nimmo probably died before the Nimmo family immigrated to the United States.

[149] *The London City and Middlesex County Directory- 1887*. London, Ont.: R. L. Polk & Co.: 1897. Pp. 216.

George, Rose Marion Nimmo's father, may have lived in Detroit for a while, but there is no record of his stay there.[150] In 1889, four years after the Nimmos left Canada, George was headed for San Francisco, California where he would stay and build a life for himself. [151] [152] [153] [154]

Marion Kerr Chalmers Nimmo surrounded by 6 of her children. Children left to right: Jean D. Nimmo (?), Mary Nimmo, Alexander Nimmo, Thomas Nimmo, Jr., Marion Chalmers Nimmo (?), and David Nimmo. Probably taken after the death of Thomas Nimmo, Sr. which was in 1903. Courtesy of Dolores Engelhardt Arden.

---

[150] There is one photograph of young George Nimmo taken in Detroit which may be evidence that he lived there. Photograph in possession of Dolores Engelhardt Arden.

[151] "Detroit City Directories, 1888-1903." *Ancestry.com* database entries for Thomas Nimmo.

[152] "United States Census, 1900." *FamilySearch.org* database entry for Thomas Nimmo.

[153] "San Francisco City Directories, 1886, 1889, 1896, 1897, 1899, 1901, 1903, 1904." *Ancestry.com* database entry for George Nimmo.

[154] "California, Voters Register, 1866-1898, San Francisco, 1892, District 29." *Ancestry.com* database entry for George Nimmo.

Thomas Nimmo. Born December 18, 1844 in Kirkliston, Scotland. Immigrated to Ontario, Canada with his wife and two children, David and George, in 1868. Immigrated to Detroit, Michigan, USA in 1885. Died July 8, 1903.

5
GEORGE AND LENA
SAN FRANCISCO, CALIFORNIA

On October 24, 1900, when he was 33 years old, George Nimmo married Lena Schnepple, who was 24, in San Francisco, California.[155] They were married at the Howard-street Methodist Episcopal Church, By Rev. Dr. John A. B. Wilson.[156]

Evidently, at 33, George, was ready to settle down permanently in San Francisco. The most of the Nimmo family had already put down roots in Detroit. David, the oldest son, had returned to Ontario, Canada.

---

[155] "Marriage Licenses. George Nimmo, 33, 1648 Hyde Street and Lena Schnepple, 24, 1108 ½ Broadway." In "Marriage Licenses." (newspaper notice) *San Francisco Call* (San Francisco, California), Tuesday, Oct. 16, 1900. Pg. 11. *Newspapers.com* database entry for George Nimmo. (Accessed: 26 Nov 2017)

[156] "Married." (newspaper notice) *The San Francisco Call*, Thursday, Oct. 25, 1900. Page 11. *Newspapers.com* database entry for Lena Schnepple. (Accessed: 27 Oct 2017) (Note: Photograph of Lena Schnepple and her bridesmaids. San Francisco. 1900. Courtesy of Dolores Engelhardt Arden.)

George and Lena Nimmo. San Francisco, California. About 1900.
Courtesy of Dolores Engelhardt Arden.

***

As early as 1888, three years after the Nimmos left Canada, the Detroit City Directory listed Thomas Nimmo, George's father, as a "mechanic", Thomas, Jr. as a "blacksmith" and George's older brother, David, as a "machinist." They were all shown as living together at 915 - 15th in Detroit.[157] [158]

In 1896, Thomas Nimmo was working in Detroit as "toolmaker," and his son, Thomas, Jr., was working as a "blacksmith." They were both living at 1285 - 24th - which was likely the Nimmo family home. The two oldest Nimmo sons, David and George, were not listed as residing or working in Detroit.[159]

In fact, George is never shown in any of the Detroit City Directories so it is hard to know if, or when, he might have ever lived or worked there. However, in an article in the San Francisco newspaper, George said, "I've been working almost since I can remember..." In the same article he said that he had worked since he was 14 and that he was a journeyman carpenter by the time he was 19 years old. George also said that he arrived in San

---

[157] "U.S. City Directories, 1822-1995." (Detroit, Michigan, City Directory, 1888). *Ancestry.com* database entry for Thomas Nimmo.

[158] Obviously, since so many of the family were living there, "915 - 15th" is the "family home." It would have been the residence of Marion Kerr Chalmers Nimmo and her daughters - as well as the working members of the family.

[159] "U.S. City Directories, 1822-1995." (Detroit, Michigan, City Directory, 1896) *Ancestry.com* database entry for Thomas Nimmo.

Francisco in 1889.[160] That means that George worked as a carpenter probably both in Ontario and in Detroit,[161] and that he was already an accomplished carpenter when he arrived in San Francisco at the age of 22.[162]

By 1892, George was listed in the San Francisco Voting Register - which describes him as 5 feet 8 inches with fair completion, blue or green eyes, and brown hair.[163] A photograph taken at the time shows George Nimmo as a good looking, confident, young man.

George always said that he came to San Francisco without a cent in his pocket - and made a success of it, which he did as he was a successful carpenter, builder, contractor and business owner in San Francisco, until he finally retired at the age of 80.[164]

---

[160] "Greeley Brought Up to Date – With a Bang." San Francisco newspaper article on Spike's (George Nimmo's) retirement at the age of 80. Published in 1946. Article in possession of Dolores Arden, but the name of the newspaper and date of publication had been removed. I have been unable to locate the original.

[161] Although George was not listed in the Detroit City Directory from 1886 through 1889, he most likely came to Detroit with the family in 1885 (as he was just 18) and, given the family work ethic, held carpenter jobs in Detroit. However, in the newspaper article, George does not say that he stayed in Detroit – only that he worked as a carpenter.

[162] In 1889, George would have had the support of the Bates family, who were still living in San Francisco, and of the Pringle family, who were still living in Oakland. John Pringle, the head of the Pringle family was a "house carpenter." Alfred Bates, head of the Bates family, was a "mechanic." Just before George Nimmo got married in 1900, the 1900 United States Census shows George was living with his relatives, the Bates family, at 324 Seventh Street, San Francisco. In: "1900, United States Census. (San Francisco, San Francisco, California)." *Ancestry.com* database entry for Mary Bates.

[163] "California, Voter Registers, 1866-1898." *Ancestry.com* database entry for George Nimmo. Photograph of George Nimmo. San Francisco. 1900 Courtesy of Dolores Engelhardt Arden.

[164] "Greeley Brought Up to Date – With a Bang." San Francisco newspaper

However, when George Nimmo met Lena Schnepple, George was working for someone else "putting in mill machinery,"[165] and Lena was a "coffee packer."[166]

Like George, Lena came from a working-class family. Throughout his life, Lena's father, Johannes Georg Schnepple,[167] had worked as a "wood turner." Lena's four brothers - George, Ernest, Robert and Frank - worked, from a very young age, at blue collar jobs. They had jobs as teamsters, postmen, ironworkers, pressman, and lithographers. The brothers, when they weren't married, generally continued to live with and support their widowed mother.[168] George Schnepple, who apparently never married, always lived with his mother.

***

Lena Schnepple Nimmo and her family. Lena's parents were both immigrants. Lena's mother, **Rosa Eichenburger**, and her family were from Bern, Switzerland. **George Schnepple**, Lena's father, was born on April 23,

---

article on Spike's retirement at the age of 80. Published in 1946. Article in possession of Dolores Arden, but the name of the newspaper and date of publication had been removed. I have been unable to locate the original.

[165] George said that he was employed putting in mill machinery before the earthquake. "Greeley Brought Up to Date – With a Bang." San Francisco newspaper article on Spike's retirement at the age of 80. Published in 1946. Article in possession of Dolores Arden, but the name of the newspaper and date of publication had been removed. I have been unable to locate the original.

[166] "1900, United States Census." (San Francisco, San Francisco, California) *Ancestry.com* database entry for Rose Schnepple.

[167] "Johannes Georg" Schnepple Americanized his name to "George"- making for a lot of "Georges" in this chapter.

[168] It seems the Schnepples struggled to get established in San Francisco. The children went to work at an early age to support their family. In: "The San Francisco City Directories for 1898 -1904." *Ancestry.com* database entries for Rosa Schnepple, George Schnepple, Robert Schnepple, Ernst Schnepple and Frank Schnepple.

1846 in Wurttemberg[169] which is located in the very southwestern part of present-day Germany.[170] [171]

The Eichenbergers/ Schnepples – Direct Line[172]

Daughter	**Rose Nimmo**	1903	San Francisco, CA
Son	**Thomas Nimmo**	1901	San Francisco, CA
Parents	George Nimmo m.	1867	Kirkliston, Scotland
	Lena Schnepple	1876	San Francisco, CA
Grandparents	**Johannes Georg Schnepple**	1846	Wurttemberg
	m. **Rosa E. Eichenberger**	1853	Bern, Switzerland
Great Grandparents	**Johannes "John" Eichenberger**	1825	Aargau, Switzerland
	m. Maria Rosina "Rosa" Kunz	1818	Aargau, Switzerland
2nd Great Grandparents	**Johann Daniel Eichenberger**	1797	Aargau, Switzerland
	m. Anna Mueller	1802	Aargau, Switzerland

---

[169] *"Wurttemberg, Germany Emigration Index." Ancestry.com* database entry for Johannes Georg Schnepple.

[170] The Kingdom of Wurttemberg existed from 1806 until 1918. And, before that, it was the Duchy of Wurttemberg which had been in existence since 1495. In: "Wurttemberg." *Wikipedia* database entry for "Wurttemberg."

[171] Information about George Schnepple sometimes indicates that he came from Wurttemberg, which was absolutely true since he emigrated before 1918. Sometimes, the source information declares George came from Germany which must reflect the later incorporation of Wurttemberg into the modern nation of Germany.

[172] Hunter, Barbara L. "Rosa Eichenberger- Hunter Wright Engelhardt Feldtman." (Ancestry Family Tree), Owner: hunterbl175. *Ancestry.com* database.

Johann Daniel Eichenberger. Rosa Eichenberger's grandfather was Johann Daniel Eichenberger. He was born on the 1st of October, 1797 in Aargau Canton, Switzerland. He was married to Anna Mueller. They had 10, or possibly 11, children, the first of whom was **Johannes "John"** Eichenberger, Rosa's father.

Children of Johann Daniel Eichenberger (1797) and Anna Mueller (1802)[173]

	Birth	Immigrated	Residence
1. Johannes "John"	1825	1864-6?[174]	Philadelphia, PA[175]
2. Anna Maria	1826	1864	Cleveland, OH
3. Rudolf Gabriel	1828		
4. Maria	1830	1854-5	Cleveland, OH
5. Daniel	1832	1865	Cleveland, OH
6. Hans Jacob	1833	?	Cleveland, OH
7. Friedrich	1835		
8. Jacob	1836	1865	Cleveland, OH
9. Elizabeth "Ela"	1839	1865	?
10.Katherine "Katarina" "Kathie"	1842	1865	Cleveland, OH

The first member of the Eichenberger family to emigrate was Maria Eichenberger with her husband, John Richner, in 1854 or 1855. They made a home in Cleveland, Ohio.

It was another 10 years before more of the Eichenberger family immigrated, and then they too went to Cleveland, Ohio. Anna Maria, and

---

[173] Hunter, Barbara L. "Johann Daniel Eichenberger - Hunter Wright Engelhardt Feldtman." (Ancestry Family Tree), Owner: hunterbl175. *Ancestry.com* database. (Note: Information is sparse for these family relationships.)

[174] "New York, Passenger Lists, 1820-1957." *Ancestry.com* database entry for John Eichenberger has a John Eichenberger of the right age and place of origin (Switzerland) arriving in New York on 16 Feb 1864.

[175] Beside the prior footnote, I have found only one other possible references to John Eichenberger before 1872. "Ohio, County Naturalization Records, 1800-1977." *Ancestry.com* database entry for John Eichenberger puts a John Eichenberger in Cuyahoga County Ohio in 1871. Otherwise, he is in Philadelphia.

her family immigrated in 1864. After the Eichenberger patriarch, Johann Daniel Eichenberger, died on December 19, 1864, Rosa's grandmother, Anna Mueller Eichenberger, and 6 more of Rosa's aunts and uncles emigrated.[176] All of these families joined Aunt Maria and Uncle John Richner in Cleveland.[177]

***

Johannes "John" Eichenberger. Johannes, Rosa Eichenberger Schnepple's father, married Maria Rosina "Rosa" Kunz in Switzerland. They had 5 children.

Children of Johannes "John" Eichenberger and Maria Rosina Kunz[178]

	Born	Immigrated[179]	Died	Location
1. Annie Marie	1851	1866	1942	Oklahoma
2. **Rosa E.**	1853	1866	1942	California
3. Johann Ernst "Ernest"	1854	1864	?	Pennsylvania
4. Berthe	1857	1866	1921	California
5. Robert	1860	1865	1945	Pennsylvania

***

In 1866, John and Rosina Eichenberger and their 5 children immigrated to the United States.[180] But instead of joining the other Eichenbergers in

---

[176] Anna Mueller Eichenberger immigrated with 4 of her children (Daniel, Jacob, Elizabeth, and Katherine) from La Havre, France to New York in December of 1865. In: "New York Passenger Lists." (1865; Arrival: New York, New York) *Ancestry.com* database entry for Daniel Eichenberger.

[177] The immigration dates for Hans Jacob Eichenberger is unknown. However, I presume that he immigrated around the same time as the rest of the family.

[178] Hunter, Barbara L. "Rosa Eichenberger, Annie Marie Eichenberger, Johann Ernst "Ernest" Eichenberger, Robert Eichenberger and Berthe Eichenberger Mann - Hunter Wright Engelhardt Feldtman." (Ancestry Family Tree), Owner: hunterbl175. *Ancestry.com* database.

[179] Immigration date as shown on the "United States Federal Census, 1900 or 1910."

[180] As you can see from the family chart, members of the family recalled

Cincinnati, they seem to have made their home in Philadelphia, Pennsylvania.[181] Perhaps there were better opportunities in Philadelphia for John Eichenberger who was a tailor - a trade was eventually taken up by both of his sons (Ernest and Robert).

Rosa, who was 13 in 1866, brought with her a "Certificate" from her teacher, Marie Lithy:

CERTIFICATE[182]

"Rosa Eichenberger from Botzberg, born 1853, attended the Second Girls' Class of the Inhabitants School at Biel. Her deportment during this time was very satisfactory and so was her work. She acquired enough knowledge, which if she will use the same, will bear good fruit. I recommend her heartily to her future teacher and my blessings go with her over the Ocean."

Biel   November 17, 1865   Marie Lithy
                                   Teacher

However, the Eichenberger family did not stay together. By 1872, John,

---

different dates for their immigration to the United States. A biography of Herbert Justin Mann states that his mother, Berthe Eichenberger "...came with her parents to Philadelphia when about seven years old..." Berthe Eichenberger Mann is Rosa Eichenberger Schnepple's sister. Berthe would have been seven in 1864. In: Tinkham, George. History of San Joaquin County. Publisher unknown, 1923. (Provided by Sheri Fenley, San Joaquin Genealogical Society)

However, a copy of a "Certificate" given to Rosa Eichenberger from her teacher in Switzerland bears the date November 17, 1865. The certificate indicated that Rosa was about to emigrate. Given the date on the certificate, if the family did emigrate together, it must have been in late 1865 (December) or early in 1866.

[181] A biography of Herbert Justin Mann states that his mother, Berthe Eichenberger "...came with her parents to Philadelphia when about seven years old..." In: Tinkham, George. *History of San Joaquin County*. Publisher unknown. 1923. (Information from Sheri Fenley, San Joaquin Genealogical Society)

[182] "Copy of Certificate given to Rosa Eichenberger." (typewritten copy) Switzerland, November 17, 1865. In possession of Beth Koller Whittenbury.

Rosa's father, had started another family with "Anna."[183]

In March of 1872, Annie Marie, Rosa's older sister, married Frederick Luthy in Cleveland, Cuyahoga, Ohio.[184] One month later, on April 20, 1872, Rosa Eichenberger married George Schnepple – also in Cuyahoga County, Ohio.[185] George Schnepple was just 3 days short of being 26 years old. Rosa Eichenberger, who was born on May 21, 1853, was almost 9 years younger than her husband, George.

The Eichenberger sons, Robert and Ernest, would stay in Philadelphia. John Eichenberger's first wife, Rosina, and his three daughters (Annie Marie, Rosa, and Berthe) and their families would eventually migrate to other states.

***

Johannes "George" Georg Schnepple. George Schnepple, Lena Schnepple Nimmo's father, must have been a young man when he immigrated to the United States because it appears that he became an American citizen in New York City on October 26, 1866, when he was only 20 years old.[186] [187]

The 1872 Cleveland, Ohio City Directory shows that George Schnepple, "wood turner," was living at 214 Broad in Cleveland, which is situated on

---

[183] Hunter, Barbara L. "Johannes Eichenberger- Hunter Wright Engelhardt Feldtman." (Ancestry Family Tree), Owner: hunterbl175. *Ancestry.com* database.

[184] Rosa's older sister, Annie Marie, married Frederick Luthy in Cleveland Ohio in March of 1872. They had one child in Cleveland in November of 1874. By 1880, they had made their way to Oklahoma. It is not clear whether the Luthy family ever went back to Philadelphia before they went to Oklahoma. In: Hunter, Barbara L. "Annie Marie Eichenberger- Hunter Wright Engelhardt Feldtman." (Ancestry Family Tree), Owner: hunterbl175. *Ancestry.com* database.

[185] "Cuyahoga County, Ohio Marriage Records and Indexes 1810-1973." *Ancestry.com* database entry for George Schnepple."

[186] "New York, Index to Petitions for Naturalization filed in New York City, 1792-1989." *Ancestry.com* database entry for George Schnepple. "California, Voter Registers, 1866-1898 (1879)." *Ancestry.com* database entry for George Schnepple.

[187] I can find no reliable information on Johannes Schnepple's parents.

Lake Erie. That means, in 1872, the Schnepples lived just across Lake Erie from Fingal, Southwold, Ontario where the Nimmos were living.[188]

By 1873, the Schnepples had moved to Philadelphia, Pennsylvania where they had a little girl on Feb 26, 1873. However, she did not survive.[189] Their second child, George Schnepple, Jr., was also born in Pennsylvania - on July 30, 1874.[190]

In 1875, Rosa along with her mother and youngest sister, Berthe traveled to Stockton, California.[191] Once in California, Berthe married Jacob Mann on the 8th of September 1875.[192] [193] Since the marriage took place shortly after the Eichenbergers and Schnepples arrived in California, one wonders whether Jacob knew the Eichenbergers and Schnepples before they arrived in California.

According to family lore, the Eichenbergers and Schnepples came to California by wagon train. Since the railroads had already spanned the continent, 1875 is very late for families to make the long trek to California by wagon. But, even at this late date, wagon trains were still in existence, and, therefore, it is possible that the family story is true.[194]

---

[188] "Cleveland, Ohio City Directory, 1872." *Ancestry.com* database entry for George Schnepple.

[189] "Pennsylvania, Philadelphia City Death Certificates" FamilySearch.org database entry for George Schnepple.

[190] "World War I Draft Registration Cards, 1917-1918." *FamilySearch.org* database entry for George Schnepple (George Schnepple, Jr.).

[191] Tinkham, George. History of San Joaquin County. Publisher unknown. 1923. (Provided by Sheri Fenley, San Joaquin Genealogical Society) (Note: Tinkham reports, "...she (Berthe) accompanied her mother and sister to Stockton.")

[192] "California, Select Marriages, 1850-1945." *Ancestry.com* database entry for Berthe Eichenberger Mann.

[193] Jacob Mann was from Wurttemberg - as was George Schnepple. Like George Schnepple, Jacob also immigrated in 1866. In: "1900, United States Federal Census." *Ancestry.com* database entry for Jacob Mann.

[194] Sheri Fenley of The San Joaquin Genealogical Society says that the wagon train to Stockton would have taken several months and cost up to $1000 in 1865 while in 1875 a train ticket for a 7-day trip from New York to San Francisco was $65. Sheri Fenley: email to Barbara Hunter. (21 Mar 2018)

Once in California, the Schnepples had five more children. Lena Schnepple was born on May 24, 1876.[195] Ernst Schnepple, who eventually was known as Earnest, was born on July 7, 1878. Frederick, who called himself "Fred" or "Frank," was born on February 27, 1880. Robert was born on September 5, 1882.[196]

Children of George Schnepple (1867) and Rosa Eichenberger (1876)

1.	Girl Infant	1873	Pennsylvania
2.	George	1874	Pennsylvania
3.	Lena	1876	California
4.	Ernst	1878	California
5.	Frederick	1880	California
6.	Robert	1882	California

In 1880, George and Rosa Schnepple were living on Grant Street, Stockton, California with 4 of their children: George, Jr., 6, Lena, 4, Ernst, 2 and Frederick, just 3 months old. The Schnepples probably lived in Stockton, California for some years because George Schnepple, Sr. is listed in Stockton Voter Registrations and California (Stockton) Great Registers from 1875 to 1884.[197]

The 1880 United States Census shows that Berthe Eichenberger Mann was living with her husband, Jacob Mann and three children in Stockton, California, just a few blocks from the Schnepples. Maria Rosina

---

[195] Information on a scrap of paper in possession of Dolores Arden says that Lena Schnepple was born on May 24th, 1874 on Vallejo Street in San Francisco. However, George Eichenberger was born on July 30, 1874 in Philadelphia so perhaps the year of Lena's birth is not quite right. On the 1880 U.S. Census, Lena's birth year is 1876.

[196] "United States Census, 1880," *Ancestry.com* database entry for George Schnepple. "United States, World War I Draft Registration Cards, 1917-1918," "World War II Draft Registration Cards, 1942" *FamiySearch.org* database entry for Robert Schnepple. "United States Census, 1900." *FamiySearch.org* database entry for Rosa Schnepple.

[197] "California, Great Registers, 1866-1910." (1880, 1882,1884) *FamiySearch.org* database entry for George Schnepple. "California, Great Registers, 1866-1910." (1876, 1879) *AncestryInstitution.com* database entry for George Schnepple.

Eichenberger, Berthe's mother, was also living with the Mann family.

But, although the Schnepple family may have lived in the Stockton area, George Schnepple always seemed to have worked and rented a room in the San Francisco Bay Area.

For example: in 1875, the year he came to California, George Schnepple is listed in the San Francisco City Directory as a "wood turner" and renting a residence in San Francisco.

The last entry for George Schnepple was in the Oakland Alameda Berkeley City Directory of 1891. At that time, George was shown working as a wood turner at the "West Berkeley Plaining Mill" and residing in San Francisco.[198]

In November of 1892 there was a death notice in the San Francisco Call. George Schnepple had died on November 2. He was only 46 years old.[199]

George Schnepple left behind a very young family when he died. His wife Rosa was just 37. George, Jr., was 18. Lena was 16; Ernest, 14; Robert, 10; and Frank, 9. Rosa Eichenberger Schnepple never seems to have worked outside the home. In 1892, George, Jr., at 18, would have been the major breadwinner for this family of five.

By 1896, the Schnepple family was living in San Francisco at 525 Lombard. The children were working. Ernest was a printer at F. Korbel & Bros. Frederick was a lithographer, and George a pressman. Rosa, at 42 years of age, was listed as a widow. Robert and Lena are not listed in the 1896 directory. George, the pressman, was 22. Ernest, the printer, was 18, and Frederick, the lithographer, was 15.[200]

In the 1900 United States Federal Census, Rosa Schnepple was the "head" of the household. Four of her children were living with her. George was a mail carrier. Robert was a salesman, and Frank was an electrician. Ernst was not shown as living with the rest of his family. Lena is at home, working as coffee packer, and about to be married to George Nimmo.[201]

---

[198] "U. S. City Directories, 1821-1989." *Ancestry.com* database entry for George Schnepple.

[199] *The San Francisco Call* - 4 Nov 1892, Fri – Pg. 8. (newspaper death notice) Newspapers.com database entry for George Schnepple.

[200] "U. S. City Directories, 1821-1989." *Ancestry.com* database entry for George Schnepple.

[201] "U. S. City Directories, 1821-1989." *Ancestry.com* database entry for George Schnepple.

***

George and Lena had their first child, Thomas, on the 17th of February 1902, in San Francisco.

Their second child, Rosa Marion Nimmo (Rose), who was probably named after both grandmothers, was born at 1107 Vallejo Street in San Francisco on the 29th of November 1903.[202]

Tom and Rose Nimmo. San Francisco. 1903.
Courtesy of Dolores Engelhardt Arden

Children of George Nimmo (1867) and Lena Schnepple (1876)

1. Thomas	1902	San Francisco, California
2. Rose	1903	San Francisco, California

By 1904, the Schnepples were in their home at 483 Buena Vista Avenue. By 1905, George, Lena, Tom and Rose Nimmo had moved into the larger of the twin house at 485 Buena Vista Avenue. The very next year, on April 18, 1906, San Francisco was devastated by an earthquake and fire. Although the earthquake and fire totally destroyed many parts of San Francisco, the handsome twin homes stood fast and housed the Nimmos and the Schnepples for many years.

---

[202] "U. S. City Directories, 1821-1989. (San Francisco, San Francisco City Directory, 1903)." *Ancestry.com* database entry for George Nimmo.

Thomas Nimmo and Rose Marion Nimmo.
San Francisco. About 1906.
Courtesy of Dolores Engelhardt Arden.

6
ROSE -
EARLY DAYS [203]

Rose Marion Nimmo's first memories may have been of the 1906 earthquake which occurred on April 18, 1906 when she was about two and a half years old.

Her home on Buena Vista Avenue had stood through the San Francisco earthquake, and, because it was high on Buena Vista Hill, it also escaped the fires that followed and which caused most of the damage to the city.

Janice Engelhardt Koller, Rose's daughter, later wrote a book[204] inspired by her mother's life in which she described the view of the fires from Buena Vista as wiggly columns of smoke rising all over the city.

The earthquake broke the City's fire mains leaving the valiant firefighters with no water to fight the fire. The Ferry Building avoided cremation only because they were able to pump water directly from the Bay to save the venerable landmark.

Many people of San Francisco lost their homes to the fire which caused more damage than the earthquake. Some of those that lost their homes evacuated across the bay. However, many stayed in the City and set up temporary living quarters on any safe space they could find, including

---

[203] The first part of Chapter 6, Rose – Early Days," is written by Rose's granddaughter, Beth Koller Whittenbury.

[204] Koller, Janice Marion Engelhardt. *The Albatross* (Unpublished manuscript). In possession of Janice's daughter, Beth Koller Whittenbury. All quotes in this chapter, unless otherwise indicated, are from Janice's book, *The Albatross*.

parks. Buena Vista Park offered one of these havens and so literally became a tent city over night. Those whose homes withstood the earthquake and fiery aftermath took in as many of these families as they could, and the Nimmos were no exception.

We don't know exactly how many families or displaced persons moved in with the Nimmos at 485 Buena Vista or how long they stayed, but Janice's book seems to indicate that multiple families moved into the basement space, and perhaps another family occupied the attic.

Stoves, which were wood or coal burning at the time, were moved outside to avoid the possibility of starting further fires. The lucky ones whose possessions withstood the fire, generously gave all they could to those who had lost everything. Again, Janice's book depicts the family giving all outgrown clothes to those living in the park who had nothing with which to clothe their children. Rose, who was kind and generous throughout her life, probably learned important lessons in perseverance, charity, and sacrifice during this time.

The indomitable nature of the City's people, many emigrant pioneers, came clear. As Janice describes it:

"For three and a half days Emmy (AKA Rose) watched the fire rage. She heard a quarter of a million people were homeless and twenty-eight thousand buildings destroyed. She knew much of her beloved city lay in ashes. San Francisco's head was bent, her people on their knees, but it was a posture not of humiliation but of faith."

When asked by his wife, in Janice's book, what would happen to San Francisco, the father in the book, who we have to assume was patterned on Rose's father, George Nimmo, replies, "Why it's our city, . . .we'll rebuild it!" And rebuild it they did. In the first 19 months after the earthquake, $90 million was spent on reconstruction.[205]

It follows that the families that moved in with the Nimmos most likely lived with them for a year or more. Thus, we have a picture of a family forced by circumstance to sacrifice greatly to help others while using their talents to help rebuild the city they had come to love.

***

---

[205] "Quick Facts about the 1906 Earthquake."
http://mceer.buffalo.edu/1906_Earthquake/additional_information/earthquake-facts.asp. (Accessed: 25 Jan 2016)

The construction boom that followed was a boon to George Nimmo's carpenter and building business. In a 1946 San Francisco newspaper article, George Nimmo, who was really called "Spike," declared, "Anybody had an opportunity after the fire - I put up a building at 345 8th Street and started in business for myself."[206] [207] In 1907, a year after the earthquake and fire, George put an ad in the San Francisco Chronicle announcing that he was a contractor and builder who could do alterations, repairs and jobbing. He would also build bricklayers' benches, mortar boards and hoists. And, he would do any and all of this work at the "lowest prices."[208] After three years George moved his business to Montgomery Street, which was in the heart of San Francisco's business district. He ran a successful business in that area for almost 40 years.

***

Another result of the earthquake was that the Nimmo's got a new neighbor, Mrs. Jennie Sturtevant Macmillan. Her family had been displaced by the earthquake. By 1908, Mrs. Macmillan, along with her mother and her grown son, Donald Macmillan, had moved into 489 Buena Vista Avenue, right next door to the Nimmos.

Mrs. Sturtevant Macmillan was from a prominent northern California pioneer family.[209] She had married Allan Dare Macmillan in a fabulous society wedding at the family home at Rancho Juanita near Ukiah in 1890. On November 5th of the following year, Jennie's only son, Donald George Macmillan was born. About 1893, Allan Dare Macmillan was no longer with the family.

---

[206] "Greeley Brought Up to Date – With a Bang." San Francisco Newspaper article on Spike's retirement at the age of 80. Published in 1946. Article in possession of Dolores Engelhardt Arden, but the name of the newspaper and date of publication had been removed.

[207] George was a hard-working man who seemed to have a knack for the contracting business. Also, one had to remember that in the early 1900's San Francisco still had a lot of vacant, buildable land. Land was still cheap and available – and George was the kind of contractor that you would hire to put up a building for you.

[208] "CONTRACT WORK WANTED." (newspaper advertisement) San *Francisco Chronicle* (San Francisco, California). Tues., Aug. 12, 1907. Pp. 9. *Newspapers.com* database entry for George Nimmo.

[209] "Party of Pioneers." Ukiah Dispatch Democrat - 18 Jun 1926. *Newspapers.com* database entry for Jennie Sturtevant Macmillan.

Jennie's brother, George Abram Sturtevant, had been the District Attorney of Mendocino County. In 1899, he became a Deputy Attorney General in San Francisco.[210] In the same year, Jennie Macmillan's father, James Hughes Sturtevant died. It is, therefore, not surprising that Jennie and the rest of the Sturtevant immediate family also moved to San Francisco.

Although she was active in San Francisco society, Mrs. Jennie Sturtevant Macmillan continued to love and to promote all things about the Ukiah community - the beauty of the land and the value of its people. She wrote enthusiastically about Ukiah in letters to the San Francisco Call and the Ukiah Daily Journal. Her actions and accomplishments were featured in both papers as well as being reported in the Ukiah Republican Press.[211]

In addition to Ukiah and its people, Jennie Sturtevant Macmillan loved and supported the arts. She attended events, such as art exhibits, concerts and such "divertissement as were featured by various social societies" - both in San Francisco and in the Ukiah area.[212] And Mrs. Jennie Sturtevant Macmillan was undoubtedly a fervent supporter of her next-door neighbor, young Rose Nimmo who loved to dance and who had the opportunity to dance at the 1915 Panama Pacific Exposition which celebrated the opening of the Panama Canal.

Much of the rubble from the fire and earthquake had been dumped into the Bay. To show the indomitable nature of her city's people, San Francisco hosted the Panama Pacific Exposition in 1915, the buildings of which were erected on that rubble. That area is now called the Marina District, and it's important to note that the District is built on fill consisting of rubble cleared from the 1906 fire and earthquake.

---

[210] George Abram Sturtevant became a Superior Court Judge in 1907. In: "Who's Who on the Pacific Coast, 1913." *Ancestry.com* database entry for George Abram Sturtevant.

[211] Article on a Luncheon with Ukiah friends. Ukiah Daily Journal, 6 Jun 1919. *Newspapers.com* database entry for Jennie Sturtevant Macmillan. Article about Jennie as a writer. Ukiah Dispatch Democrat, 1 Jan 1932. *Newspapers.com* database entry for Jennie Sturtevant Macmillan. Article on a Visit to Ukiah. Ukiah Dispatch Democrat, 12 Sep 1913. *Newspapers.com* database entry for Jennie Sturtevant Macmillan.

[212] Macmillan, Jennie Sturtevant. "San Francisco Letter." Ukiah Dispatch Democrat – 3 Mar 1916. Newspapers.com database entry for Jennie Sturtevant Macmillan.

For Rose those foundations supported her love of dance. At twelve, she was an accomplished ballerina, enough so that she danced on the stage of the Palace of Fine Arts during the 1915 Panama Pacific Exposition when she was twelve years old.[213]

***

Despite the disruption caused by the earthquake, young Rose probably enjoyed a typical San Francisco childhood. She had a "stay-at-home" mother[214] and a father who went off to work – probably in the family automobile – a Ford.[215]

Rose and the Gang. Rose is on the far left. Her brother, Tom, is the boy on the left. Buena Vista Park, San Francisco. About 1912. Courtesy of Dolores Engelhardt Arden.

Youngsters in the immediate neighborhood would have formed a congenial group that included the neighborhood children of all ages - who played together and created their own games and entertainment.[216]

---

[213] Rose appears to be about 15 years old in this picture. About 1918. Courtesy of Dolores Engelhardt Arden.

[214] "Greeley Brought Up to Date – With a Bang." San Francisco Newspaper article on Spike's retirement at the age of 80. Published in 1946. Article in possession of Dolores Engelhardt Arden, but the name of the newspaper and date of publication had been removed.

[215] The Nimmo family owned one car, a Ford Model T or A, which George Nimmo drove. Dolores Engelhardt Arden: email to Barbara Hunter. (3 Apr 2018)

[216] I'm just remembering how it was when I grew up in San Francisco one generation later. We all grew up in an era of one-car families - without

For example, young Rose also probably found amusement building makeshift sleds from scraps left from her father's business and sliding down the steep grassy hillside which formed the vacant lot next to the Buena Vista houses. As Janice describes it in her book:

"Emmy and Hans went into the dark basement beneath the house. On one side was a pile of boxes and orange crates. They rummaged through them until they found two suitable as sleds. They nailed a narrow board lengthwise along the underside of the boxes to form runners. Then Emmy got two pieces of rope from Papa's workbench and attached one piece to the front of each sled."

On quiet evenings, Rose, like many girls her age, worked on her embroidery.

When money allowed, young Rose probably begged to go down the Chutes, a famous water toboggan located at 10th Avenue and Fulton from 1902-1907 and later relocated to Fillmore Street when it became the center of the City's commercial district during the reconstruction after the quake. Children could ride the Chutes for 5 cents and adults for 10 cents.

Typically, family members would also frequently visit each other as part of the social activities of the time. Such activities generally would not cost much money. For example, the Nimmo family would cross the Bay on occasion to hike Mt. Tamalpais, or they picnicked closer to home in Golden Gate Park which had been created in the late 1800's.

***

In 1915, there was a special visit by Thomas Nimmo, Jr., his wife, Phoebe Neuman Nimmo, and their daughter, Violet, who came all the way from Detroit. They probably saw Rose dance at the Panama Pacific Exposition. This special visit was commemorated in several photographs.[217] The visit also had quite unexpected and quite lasting consequences because

---

computers and cell phones – and without much spending money. We made our own toys and entertainment and "paled" with everyone on the block. I can't imagine it being much different for Rose and her brother, Tom. Photograph of Rose and the neighborhood gang. San Francisco. About 1913. Courtesy of Dolores Engelhardt Arden.

[217] It is likely they had initially come to San Francisco to view the Panama Pacific Exposition – and to see Rose dance. I'm sure they must have stayed with Rose's family.

Violet Nimmo probably met Rose's next-door neighbor – the handsome Donald George Macmillan - during this visit.[218]

Top Row (L to R): The Thomas Nimmo, Jr. Family: Prock, Thomas, and Violet. Bottom Row (L to R) Rose, Tom and Lena Nimmo. Marin County, California. 1915. Courtesy of Dolores Engelhardt Arden.

***

The World War, subsequently called World War I, impacted everyone - including the Nimmos. Rose participated in Red Cross marches and her uncles on the Schnepple side registered for the draft. However, we have no record that anyone in the Nimmo or Schnepple family fought in WWI. On the other hand, Donald Macmillan, who was born in 1890, was a sergeant in the Marines.

At the end of the war, in 1919, Donald Macmillan returned from France, and Violet Nimmo, who had gone to the University of Michigan, transferred to the University of California.[219] [220] Her parents, Phoebe and

---

[218] It is just my supposition that Violet Nimmo met Donald Macmillan in 1915. But, since Donald was residing with his mother right next door to the Nimmo's in 1915, it very likely that they first met at that time.

[219] "U.S., School Yearbooks, 1880-2012"; Yearbook Title: The Michiganensian Yearbook; Year: 1917, 1918. " Ancestry.com database entry for Violet Nimmo.

Thomas Nimmo Jr. had also moved - but they had moved to southern California where Thomas Nimmo Jr. was the owner of a car repair business.[221]

No doubt Violet Nimmo spent a lot of time at her cousin Rose's house on Buena Vista while she was attending the University of California. Rose, Violet Nimmo, Donald Macmillan, Claude Grant (who boarded with Mrs. Macmillan), "Brooksie," and "Frank" formed a group that Rose dubbed the "Buena Vista Sextet." Rose was still a teenager at this time. The rest of the members of the Sextet were older - some, like Donald Macmillan, considerably older, but it appears that they were all great friends.

"The Famous Sextet from Buena Vista." Top L to R: Rose, Frank, Brooksie, and Claud. Bottom: Donald Macmillan and Violet Nimmo. Buena Vista Avenue, San Francisco. 1920's. Courtesy of Dolores Engelhardt Arden.

On November 5th, 1920, Violet (who had just graduated from UC, Berkeley) announced her engagement to Donald Macmillan at "a charming dinner at the Fairmount Hotel on her fiancée's birthday, ..."[222] Violet and Donald were married in 1921.[223]

---

[220] "Donald Macmillan to Wed Los Angles Girl." (newspaper article) Ukiah Dispatch Democrat, 3 Dec 1920, Fri, Page 4. *Newspapers.com* database entry for Violet Nimmo.

[221] "1930 United States Federal Census. (Los Angeles, Los Angeles, California)" *Ancestry.com* database entry for Thomas Nimmo.

[222] "Donald Macmillan to Wed Los Angles Girl." (newspaper article) Ukiah Dispatch Democrat, 3 Dec 1920, Fri, Page 4. *Newspapers.com* database entry for Violet Nimmo.

[223] As of now, I have no record of the actual marriage which I assume took place the following year - 1921.

In just a few years, they would move to Sanal near Ukiah in northern California where they would run a hotel.[224] But, as Mrs. Jennie Sturtevant Macmillan remained living next door to the Nimmos, Donald and Violet must have continued to be in frequent touch with Rose and her family.

Violet Nimmo Macmillan, Donald Macmillan and Rose Nimmo. San Francisco. 1920's. Courtesy of Dolores Engelhardt Arden.

***

As a flapper in the twenties, Rose had lots of fun. Cars were a relatively new invention, but we have pictures of her driving several. We even have a picture of her trying out a motorcycle.

Rose and Fred. Buena Vista Avenue, San Francisco. About 1922. Courtesy of Dolores Engelhardt Arden.

***

While Rose was being a flapper, Rose's brother, Tom, went to sea at 18. He turned 18 on February 17th, 1920, and, just two months later, Tom applied for a Seaman's Protection Certificate so he could sail out of San

---

[224] "1930 United States Federal Census, (Sanel, Mendocino, California)" *Ancestry.com* database entry for Donald Macmillan.

Francisco aboard the Moshulu.[225] By 1922, the San Francisco City Directory still listed Tom as a seaman.[226]

Two years later, Tom had met and married Josephine Ferrero who was from an Italian immigrant family that lived in the Mission District of San Francisco.[227] Tom and "Joe" had had a daughter, Phyllis, on 7th of October 1924. At that time, they were living in Oakland, and Tom was earning a living as an iron worker.

Josephine Ferrero Nimmo, "Joe," and daughter, Phyllis. San Francisco. 1925.
Courtesy of Dolores Engelhardt Arden.

---

[225] Because of the 1906 fire, Tom did not have his required birth certificate. Instead, both of his parents, George and Lena, were required to attest to his birth.

[226] "U.S., Applications for Seaman's Protection Certificates, 1916-1940." *Ancestry.com* database entry for Thomas Nimmo.

[227] There was a connection between the Ferreros and the Schnepples which may have been where and how Tom Nimmo met his wife, Josephine Ferrero. Frank Schnepple, who was Rose's and Tom's uncle, married Hazel Pfortner. Hazel's much younger sister, Elaine, married John Ferrero, Josephine Ferrero Nimmo's brother. Then Josephine Ferrero married Tom Nimmo.

***

When she graduated from Poly (Polytechnic) High School, Rose went to work for the Neville Book Company as a stenographer- a job she very much enjoyed. She also continued a satisfying social life with her many friends. However, in or about 1924, Rose's life would change forever with the introduction of a new person in her life who she would call "Bobby Dear."

BARBARA L. HUNTER

7
"BOBBY DEAR"

Rose Marion Nimmo fell in love with Robert Caspar Engelhardt. Everyone called him "Bob," except Rose. Rose, who thought Bob was very, very special, called him "Bobby, Dear."[228] [229]

Bob was a sweet, gentle man who cherished Rose. He thought Rose's strength, courage, vivaciousness and charm quite wonderful.[230] Bob had a terrific voice. When they were courting, Bob and Rose would sing "Tea for Two" and mean every word.[231]

---

[228] "Bobby Dear" is the title of the photograph of Bob Engelhardt in an album created and titled by Rose Nimmo Engelhardt. Rose's photograph album in possession of Dolores Arden.

[229] Rose also called Bob, "Bobby Dear" in letters to Bob and told him he was very dear to her. Unpublished letters in possession of Dolores Engelhardt Arden.

[230] Unpublished letters from Bob to Rose. Letters in possession of Dolores Engelhardt Arden.

[231] Unpublished letter from Bob Engelhardt to his wife, Rose. Letters in possession of Dolores Arden.

Beth Koller Whittenbury recalls:

"Bob was fun to be around. I never met him, but my Mom always talked about how he had a great sense of humor and a contagious laugh. In fact, she likened it to that scene in Mary Poppins where they are all laughing so hard that they started floating up to the ceiling. My Mom said her Dad would start to laugh and then everyone else would soon be in hysterics, but not really know what was so funny that it had started him laughing in the first place."[232]

Like Rose, Bob was a native San Franciscan.[233] He was born on December 28, 1900 at the Engelhardt's home, which was an apartment at 7 Post Court, in San Francisco, California.[234] He was so little when he was born that his mother first kept him in a cigar box filled with cotton wool.[235]

At the time of Bob's birth there were 4 other people living in the

---

[232] Beth Koller Whittenbury: email to Barbara Hunter. (December 2017)

[233] Bob Engelhardt's signed "Application for Seaman's Protection Certificate." Sworn to 31st day of January, 1919 in San Francisco, California. To substantiate Bob's claim of United States citizenship, Bob's father, Alex Engelhardt swore that he (Alex) had been a resident of San Francisco for 20 years, that he was Bob's father, and that he had known Bob for 18 years. In: "U.S. Applications for Seaman's Protection Certificates, 1916-1940." *Ancestry.com* database entry for Oswald Engelhardt. (Note: Bob's file does not seem to be indexed on Ancestry in a way that allows direct access to Bob's "Application for Seaman's Protection Certificate" file and must be accessed by searching Ancestry for the file of Bob's older brother, Oswald Engelhardt, and electronically paging back to Bob's file which is after Oswald's file in the "Applications for Seaman's Protection Certificate's.")

[234] "1900, United States Federal Census" (San Francisco, San Francisco, California) *Ancestry.com* database entry for Alex Engelhardt. (Note: If you try to locate Post Court today, it can't be found. In the census, it is between a building at 962 Post Street and a building at 968 Post Street in San Francisco. Neither Post Court or those other addresses on Post Street still exist. However, on the opposite side of the street there still is a narrow, short side street/court called Meacham. I expect "Port Court" was the same sort of street/court.)

[235] Helen Hunter: as told to her daughter, Barbara Hunter.

Engelhardt apartment on Post Court: Bob's father, **Alexander Gustave Engelhardt**; his mother, **Sophia Feldtmann Engelhardt**; Bob's older brother, Oswald Kaspar Engelhardt;[236] and Bob's young uncle, Earnest[237] Feldtmann, who was just 15 when Bob was born.[238] Bob's sister, Helen Elsie Engelhardt, was far in the future.[239]

The Engelhardts: Robert, Sophia, Oswald and Alexander.
San Francisco. About 1915.
Owned by Barbara Hunter

---

[236] "Oswald" was pronounced "OS-VALT." – per Oswald's sister, Helen Engelhardt Hunter as told to Barbara Hunter.

[237] "Earnest" – as spelled on the 1900 United States Federal Census for San Francisco. It is my understanding from the Texas Feldtmans that "Earnest" was the original spelling. Generally, Earnest, who is Sophia Feldtman's brother, spelled his name "Ernest."

[238] "1900, United States Federal Census.' (San Francisco, San Francisco, California). *Ancestry.com* database entry for Alexander Engelhardt.

[239] Helen Elsie Engelhardt was born at home in San Francisco on January 5, 1916.

Perhaps, with the new baby, there was a need for new quarters because, by 1901, the Engelhardts had moved to an apartment on the corner of Post and Hyde Street (705 Hyde) where they stayed until 1905. However, by 1901, Bob's Uncle Earnest was not with the Engelhardts, Earnest had gone back to San Antonio, Texas.

Children of Alexander Gustave Engelhardt and Sophia Feldtmann

1. Oswald Kaspar Engelhardt   1 May 1896   San Antonio, TX
2. **Robert Caspar Engelhardt**   28 Dec 1900   San Francisco, CA
3. Helen Elsie Engelhardt   5 Jan 1916   San Francisco, CA

***

Bob's father, Alexander Gustave Engelhardt,[240] was born on March 15, 1867 in Leipzig, Germany. He came the United States in 1893 – when he was 26 years old.[241] [242] According to family lore, Alexander, who was called "Alex," suddenly had an opportunity to go to America with a friend. He went home, packed and left for the United States the next day.[243] Although there is no official record of Alex's departure[244] or his arrival, we do know his ship traveled through the Straights of Gibraltar. Alex must have even

---

[240] In the San Francisco city directories, Alexander Engelhardt's middle name is generally Gustave or "G." But sometime Alexander uses "A" or "August" as his middle name. He is also generally known by "Alex" not "Alexander."

[241] Since Alex Engelhardt was born in Germany on March 15, 1867, he was 26 when he arrived in the United States. "1900 United States Federal Census for Alex Engelhardt, (San Francisco, San Francisco, California)." *Ancestry.com* database entry for Alexander Engelhardt.

[242] Helen Engelhardt's (Helen Engelhardt Hunter's) birth certificate (in possession of Barbara Hunter) states that Alex, Helen's father, is born in "Berlin, Germany." On Oswald Engelhardt's "Application for Seamen's Protection Certificate," which Alex Engelhardt swore to and signed, Alex lists "Leipzig, Germany" as his place of birth – and so does the doctor (Sigmund Berg) who certified Oswald's birth.

[243] Helen Engelhardt Hunter: as told to her daughter, Barbara Hunter.

[244] The envelope containing the souvenir scarf says, "Silk handkerchief from Gibraltar bought there in 1893 coming over from Gemma Italy."

stopped in Gibraltar as he bought a souvenir scarf that is retained in the family to this day.[245]

In emigrating, Alex left behind his mother, father and other family members whose names are not known, but are pictured as the "Famlie Engelhardt."[246] [247] Bob might never have seen his Engelhardt grandparents, but he must have known their names[248] since Bob certainly was told that his grandfather was an opera singer.[249] None of the family ever questioned this statement as Bob's father, Alex, had a beautiful voice and sang "light opera" in performances given by the local German societies, both in San Antonio and San Francisco.[250]

---

[245] Envelop and scarf retained by Alex's granddaughter, Barbara Hunter.

[246] "Famlie Engelhardt" is a series of small photograph pasted on heavy board and labeled "Famlie Engelhardt." In possession of Barbara Hunter.

[247] Helen Hunter said that she recalled some Engelhardts from Germany visiting her family, but she was vague as to who they were- possibly because it happened when she was a young child. The visitors possibly could have been some Engelhardts of the younger generation that immigrated. According to Helen Hunter, the older generation of Engelhardts who were still living in Germany had sent a set of silverware as a wedding present.

[248] Given German naming patterns, it is quite possible that Bob's grandfather was named Oswald Engelhardt.

[249] Helen Engelhardt Hunter: as told to her daughter Barbara Hunter.

[250] Many newspaper stories including: "At Beethoven Hall." (newspaper article) The Daily Light. (San Antonio Texas) Monday, October 18, 1897. "German Day at Shell Mound Park." (newspaper article) San Francisco Chronicle (San Francisco, California). 01 Oct 1911, pp 48. *genealogybank.com* database entry for Alex Engelhardt. "The Committee Plans Special Excursion to Fresno During

These two photographs are part of a photo montage of the "Famlie Engelhardt – 1910." These two pictures are the middle two photographs in a montage of 9 photographs. I believe that they are either Alexander Engelhardt's parents or grandparents. From the date of the picture, the type of clothing and the approximate age of the people in the photograph, these are probably Alex Engelhardt's parents, and, therefore, Bob Engelhardt's grandparents. "Famlie Engelhardt" in possession of Barbara Hunter.

Interstate Fair There." (newspaper article) San Francisco Chronicle (San Francisco, California). 29 Sep 1911, pp 3. *genealogybank.com* database entry for Alex Engelhardt.

Alex Engelhardt as the "Good Dwarf" and "Louise"[251] as the "Mean Queen" performing in Snow White and the 7 Dwarves. "Our Theater Group Photograph" taken in Magdeburg, Germany. Early 1880's.[252]

By 1894, less than a year after he emigrated from Germany, Alex was in San Antonio. Why Alex came to San Antonio, Texas isn't known. However, San Antonio had a large German community, and it is very possible that Alex already had friends, or even family, there.

Alex was a jeweler and a watchmaker all his life. It seems that he already possessed those skills when he came to the United States because, by 1894, he was already working as a watchmaker for A. Sartor, a San Antonio jeweler.[253]

---

[251] On the back of the photograph only "Louise" and "Alex" are noted so perhaps "Louise" is Alex's sister.

[252] Translation from German by JoAnn Elizabeth Seibert and Ingrid Brandt.

[253] "San Antonio, Texas City Directories, 1891-94, (San Antonio City Directory, 1891)." *Ancestry.com* database entry for Alexander Engelhardt.

And, not surprisingly, Alex boarded with a German speaking family - at 420 Garden Avenue in San Antonio - the home of Caspar Georg Feldtmann, Anna Albrecht Feldtman and their large, lively family.

Caspar Georg Feldtmann.
Possession of Barbara Hunter

Anna Albrecht Feldtmann.
Possession of Barbara Hunter

Caspar and Anna Feldtmann had 10 children, one of which, Elizabeth, was less than one year old when she died in 1880.[254] The rest of the children were still living in the San Antonio area in 1894.

Children of Caspar Georg Feldtmann and Anna Albrecht

1.	Louise "Lou"	1869 - 1945
2.	Maria Anne "Annie"	1871 - 1940
3.	Alexander P.	1873 - 1911
4.	Oscar	1875 - 1926

---

[254] Elizabeth died of "Chronic Diarrhoea" (sic) on Oct 13, 1880. She was 7 months old. In: San Antonio Municipal Archives: "Elisabeth Feldtmann - Death Records 1880-1885." San Antonio.gov/Municipal ArchivesSearch. Pg. 11. (Accessed: 27 Jan 2018)

5.	Sophia "Sophie"	**1877 - 1942**
6.	Elizabeth "Lisbeth"	1880 - 1880
7.	Mary	1881 - 1965
8.	Katherine Louise "Kate"	1883 - 1964
9.	Earnest	1885 - 1950
10.	George Caspar	1888 – 1953

The two oldest girls, Lou and Annie, were married and living with their own families. The oldest daughter, Bob's Aunt Lou, had married Isadore Cahen in 1890.[255] Bob's Aunt Annie, the second oldest Feldtmann child, had married William Deussen the next year, 1891.[256]

In 1894, the other 7 Feldtmann children still lived at home. Alexander, 21 years old, was a carpenter.[257] Oscar, 20 years old, was a plumber.[258]

The next oldest child, Sophia Feldtmann, was just 17 - beautiful and vivacious. In 1894, *The Daily Light*, a San Antonio newspaper, had a long article on the Turn-Verein Picnic which the paper described as "A Good Old-Fashioned Picnic, with Athletic Games, Dancing, Romping and Mirth."[259] Sophia was the winner of the 100 yard (dash?) in the lady's class. She won a cup and saucer.[260]

---

[255] "1900 United States Federal Census." (San Antonio Ward 5, Bexar, Texas) *Ancestry.com* database entry for Louise Feldtmann.

[256] "1900 United States Federal Census." (Justice Precinct 5, Bexar, Texas) *Ancestry.com* database entry for Annie Feldtmann.

[257] "San Antonio, Texas City Directory, 1895." *Ancestry.com* database entry for Alexander Feldtmann.

[258258] "U.S. City Directories, 1822-1995." (San Antonio, City Directory, 1895) *Ancestry.com* database entry for Oscar Feldtmann.

[259] "Turn-Verein Picnic." *San Antonio Light*. (newspaper article) Monday, May 7, 1894.

[260] "Turn-Verein Picnic." *San Antonio Light*. (newspaper article) Monday, May 7, 1894.

Alex Engelhardt's activities were also in "The Daily Light." With his beautiful voice, he was featured in the "theatrical entertainment" of the German Dramatic Club of San Antonio.[261]

***

Alexander Gustave Engelhardt.

Alex Engelhardt fell in love with Sophia Feldtmann. A marriage was "arranged."[262] On August 12, 1895, the engagement was announced in *The Daily Light*. Sophia was described as "one of San Antonio's favorite pets." Alex was "the chief manipulator of 'Wheels' at Sartor's jewelry" store.[263]

On the 28th of November 1895, Alex and Sophie were married by A. C. Ulrich at Saint John's Lutheran Church. Alex was 28. Sophie was 18.[264]

***

---

[261] "German Dramatic Club." (newspaper announcement) *The Daily Light*. (Duplicate Copy- no date apparent).

[262] Helen Engelhardt Hunter was very clear in a story to her daughter, Barbara Hunter, that her mother, Sophia Feldtmann Engelhardt had an "arranged" marriage.

[263] "Engaged." (newspaper announcement) *The Daily Light*. Monday, August 12, 1985.

[264] "Texas, Marriages, 1837-1973." *FamilySearch.org* database entry for A. Engelhardt and Sophie Feldtmann.

Caspar George Feldtmann,[265] a well-known San Antonio merchant,[266] was a Swiss immigrant.[267] He had come to the United States from Glarus, Switzerland where his family had been living for generations.[268]

Sophia's mother, Anna Albrecht just missed being an immigrant as she is said to have been born on board ship - just as the ship carrying her family, the Albrechts, landed in Indianola, Texas.[269] Anna was born on

---

[265] Caspar George Feldmann changed his name to "Feldtmann" by adding the "t." Early in Caspar's life in the United States, the spelling of "Feldmann/Feldtmann" is inconsistent. For example, Caspar is "Feldmann" on the 1870 United States Federal Census and "Feldtmann" on the 1880 United States Federal Census. His father's family in Switzerland goes by "Feldmann."

[266] "C. G. Feldtmann." (San Antonio newspaper obit) *San Antonio Express* Volume XLI, Issue 29, Pp. 7. *Genealogybank.com* database entry for Caspar Feldtman.

[267] Although Caspar Georg Feldtmann's family had been in Glarus, Switzerland for several generations (per research by Jody Rippel Feldtman Wright, Robert Feldtman, Fern Feldtman Fahnert, and others), over the years Caspar Georg Feldtmann gave several locations for his birth. For example, in information given to the Veteran's Home of California where he stayed for the last years of his life, Caspar said his place of birth was Russia. He claimed the same thing on the 1900, United States Federal Census. However, on the 1880 United States Federal Census, Caspar said he was born in Switzerland and that his mother was born in Russia. In a Xerox copy of handwritten "Declaration of Intention to become a Citizen of the United States," County Court, County of Kendall, State of Texas. Signed 6th day of August,1867, Caspar said that he was born in Glarus, Switzerland. (Researched by Jody Feldtmann Wright, San Antonio Texas, 1985) There are more examples, but the answers to Caspar's place of birth vary between Russia and Switzerland. Caspar was, no doubt, a citizen of Switzerland.

[268] Family genealogy charts and research by the Feldtman Family, including research by Jody Rippel Feldtman Wright, Fern Feldtman Fahnert, Robert Feldtman, and Katy Feldtman.

[269] Sandra Fahnert Stacy: family lore in email to Barbara Hunter. (Note: All available sources, including the United States Federal Census, state that Anna Albrecht Feldtman's birth place is Texas, but, currently, nothing in the sources,

Christmas Day, 25th of December 1850[270] - a Christmas present for her parents: **Carl Heinrich "Charles" Albrecht** and **Henriette Dorothee Louise Kaufmann "Louise" Albrecht.**[271]

Children of "Charles" Albrecht and "Louise" Kaufmann[272]

1. Ferdinand August   1846
2. Charles   1847
3. Emil Herrmann   1848
4. William F.   1848
5. **Anna**   1850
6. Elise/Eliera   1853

***

As with many German and Swiss immigrants, Caspar George Feldtmann must have come to United States with the intention of enlisting in the Union Army - for, within 10 days of when he landed, he had joined the New York Light Artillery. Caspar was 18 at the time.

In his "Declaration of Intention to become a Citizen," Caspar Georg Feldtmann swears:

"that he immigrated to the United States and arrived at the port of New York in the State of New York in or about the 27th day of January 1862, that he enlisted in the army of the United States in or about the 5th of February 1862, and was honorably discharged the 6th of September 1865."[273]

---

including her death certificate, lists "Indianola, Texas" as Anna's birthplace.

[270] "Anna Feldtmann - Texas Department of State Health Services; Austin Texas, USA." "Texas Death Certificates, 1903–1982. " *Ancestry.com* database entry for Anna Feldtmann.

[271] "C. H. Albrecht et. al Proof of Heirship to Feldtmann and Albrecht." (Photocopy of partial document from Sheila Feldtman to Sandy Fahnert Stacy to Barbara Hunter.) Per the document "Louisa Albrecht" died in 1858 when her daughter Anna was only 8 years old. (Carl Albrecht married again. Anna is a child from his first marriage.)

[272] Ibid. "C. H. Albrecht et. al Proof of Heirship to Feldtmann and Albrecht."

[273] "Declaration of Intention to become a Citizen of the United States," (Printed copy) County Court, County of Kendall, State of Texas. Signed 6th day of

Caspar fought in the Civil War for 2 ½ years. It appears that Caspar first was a private with the 2nd Independent Battery, New York Light Artillery.[274] Then he reenlisted on the 1st of July 1863 at Fort Lyon, Virginia, into Company K of the New York 15th Heavy Artillery Regiment - again as a private.[275] He was promoted to 2nd Lieutenant on the 10th of September 1864 and transferred from K Company to L Company one day later - on September 11, 1864.[276] Then, Caspar was promoted to 1st Lieutenant on the 17th day of June 1865 and transferred from L company to B company on the same day.[277]

During his time in the service Caspar fought in many of the major engagements of the Civil War: "Richmond, Chancellorsville, Gettysburg, Wilderness, Spotsylvania, Cold Harbor and Petersburt (sic)."[278]

Casper Feldtmann mustered out in Washington, D.C. on the 22nd day of August 1865. From there, he made his way to San Antonio's German community where he met his future wife, Anna Albrecht. Caspar Georg Feldtmann married Anna Albrecht on August 11, 1868 in Boerne, Kendall County, Texas.[279] [280]

August, 1867. "Declaration of Intention to become a Citizen" – original in possession of Jody Feldtman Wright. (Researched by Jody Feldtman Wright, San Antonio Texas, 1985.)

[274] "U.S Civil War Soldiers, 1861-1865." *AncestryInstitution.com* database entry for Caspar Feldtmann.

[275] "Caspar Feldmann in the U.S., Civil War Soldier Records and Profiles, 1861-1865." *Ancestry.com* database entry for Caspar Feldmann. (Note: Caspar Feldtmann's name is spelled several ways. I always try to show the spelling as it is written in a particular source. This source is accessed under "Feldmann."

[276] "The American Civil War Research Database" *Alexanderstreet.com* database entry for Caspar Feldtmann (or Caspar Feldmann), Union Army.

[277] Ibid. "The American Civil War Research Database."

[278] Information taken from February 14, 2005 letter to Barbara Hunter from Carol Bell of the Museum Archives of the Veterans Home of California where Caspar Georg Feldtmann resided from 1903 until his death on the 19th of January, 1906.

[279] With my northwestern accent it is impossible to get the right pronunciation, but, to me, "Boerne" sounds like "Bernie."

The Feldtmann Family.
Parents: Anna Albrecht Feldtmann and Caspar Georg Feldtmann.
The older children (L to R): Oscar, "Annie," "Lou," Alexander.
The baby is Elizabeth.
Sophia is front and center.
1880.
Picture used with permission of Katy Feldtman

---

[280] "United States Federal Census, 1900." (San Antonio Ward 8, Bexar, Texas, 1900) *Ancestry.com* database entry for Caspar Feldtmann. And private family tree information which included a restatement of information from the Feldtmann/Albrecht marriage license which can be found at the Kendall County Court House, Boerne, Kendall, Texas.

Bob Engelhardt would have been told many stories[281] about his grandfather, Caspar Feldtmann, and his Swiss family:

- that Caspar Georg Feldtmann was the son of a noble man.
- that the Feldtmanns lived near (or lived in a "castle" near) Napoleon Bonaparte's brother's "castle."
- that Caspar was born in Russia – St. Petersburg, Russia - while his mother was visiting her family there.
- that not only was Caspar's father a nobleman, he was also a famous painter.
- that Caspar came to America to seek his fortune because, not being the first-born son, he would not inherit anything from his father.

How much of this family lore is true? First, it is true that Caspar Georg Feldmann was not the family's first-born son. His parents, **Kaspar Georg von Feldmann** (1805-1866) and **Sophie Henriette Harmsen** (1817-1883), had 6 children. Bob's grandfather, Caspar Georg, was the second son in the von Feldmann family.[282]

However, the family chart also shows that a first-born son, also called "Kaspar," died when he was about two.[283] Although Caspar George had had an older brother, when Caspar George Feldmann came to America in 1862, he would have been the oldest living son of the von Feldtmann family.

---

[281] As told to Barbara Hunter by her mother, Helen Engelhardt Hunter – but also as discussed with Texas cousins: Gail Noonan Fordyce and Sandra Fahnert Stacy.

[282] Most of the Feldtman genealogy has been done by members of the Feldtman Family (including research by Jody Rippel Feldtman Wright, Fern Feldtman Fahnert, George Feldtman, Jr., Robert Feldtman, Sandy Fahnert Stacy, Katy Feldtmann, Sheila Feldtman, and many, many others). My recording of this genealogy can be found on *Ancestry.com* in the Hunter Wright Engelhardt Feldtman Family Tree. Owner: hunterbl175. (Note: According to family research, Kaspar von Feldmann was divorced from Sophia Henriette Harmsen in 1856.)

[283] Presumably, when Bob's grandfather, Caspar Feldmann, was born in 1843, he was given the name of his older brother who had died in 1840. This was a typical practice at that time.

Children of Kaspar Georg von Feldmann
& Sophia Henriette Harmsen

1.	Sophia Elisabeth	1836 - 1837
2.	Kaspar Feldtman	1839 - 1840
3.	Olga Amalia	1840 - 1842
4.	Sophia Amalia	1842 -
5.	**Caspar G. "Kaspar G."**	**1843 - 1906**
6.	Heinrich Alexander Wilhelm	1845 – 1865

Was Caspar's father a nobleman? Caspar's father was called "von Feldmann"[284] so that could mean he had standing in his country. As he is the only one of any Feldmann generation called "von Feldmann," it was probably an honorary title and could not be inherited.

The existence of Napoleon Bonaparte's brother's castle that was located near the Feldmann family home remains a mystery.

Was Caspar born in Russia? On various documents, Bob's grandfather, Caspar Georg Feldmann indicated that he was born in Russia and/or his mother was from Russia.[285] [286] [287]

---

[284] Previously cited. Research by Feldtman Family.

[285] "1870 United States Federal Census." (San Antonio Ward 3, Bexar, Texas.) (Birthplace Russia) *Ancestry.com* database entry for Caspar Feldtmann." In a letter from The Veteran's Home of California. Caspar stated he was born in Russia. He claimed the same thing on the 1900, United States Federal Census. However, on the 1880 United States Federal Census, Caspar said he was born in Switzerland and that his mother was born in Russia. In a Xerox copy of handwritten "Declaration of Intention to become a Citizen of the United States," County Court, County of Kendall, State of Texas. Signed 6th day of August,1867. (Researched by Jody Feldtmann Wright, San Antonio Texas, Research: 1985), Caspar said that he was born in Glarus, Switzerland. There are more examples, but the answers to Caspar's place of birth vary between Russia and Switzerland. Caspar was, no doubt, a citizen of Switzerland. Compilation of Family History (including "Feldmann." (an unpublished research paper, no date) by Jody Rippel Feldtman Wright and Fern Feldtman Fahnert states that "Sophia Henrietta Harmsen was from Lubeck, in Northern Germany."

[286] My Ancestry DNA test indicated that I'm over a ¼ eastern European. I believe that the only source of this DNA would be from my Engelhardt - Feldtmann family – perhaps from the "Russian" mother of Caspar Feldtmann.

Initially, it does seem likely that Caspar was born while his mother was away from home. However, in Caspar Georg Feldtmann's "Declaration of Intention to become a Citizen of the United States," he states:

"that he is the natural born subject of the Republic of Switzerland, that he is born in Glarus – that he is twenty-three years old." The document was signed on August 6, 1867 by "Gaspard Feldtmann."[288]

Was Caspar's father a painter? In addition to being a successful business man, Caspar's father, Kaspar von Feldmann, seemed to have been a painter of some repute. Caspar's father mentioned in two books on Swiss artists.[289] [290] A translation of the German text from Neue Zurcher Zeitun says that von Feldmann of Glarus was born there in 1805. First, he was a salesman in Petersburg, and later he privatized (formed his own business) in

---

[287] Compilation of Family History (including "Feldmann.") (no date) by Jody Rippel Feldtman Wright and Fern Feldtman Fahnert (Note on research document: "This information was gathered from recorded documents in Glarus, Switzerland, which were brought by a friend to George Feldtman of DeRidder, La.; also from photocopies of official documents and records gathered by Fern Feldtman Fahnert; and national archive military records obtained by Jody Rippel Feldtman Wright.").

[288] Copy of handwritten "Declaration of Intention to become a Citizen of the United States," County Court, County of Kendall, State of Texas. Signed 6th day of August,1867. (Researched by Jody Feldtmann Wright, San Antonio Texas, 1985)

[289] "FELDMANN (Kaspar), peintre d'architecture et paysagiste, ne a Glarus en 1805, mort a Stuttgart en 1866 (Ec. Suis.).   Feldmann fut commercant et n'eut d'autre prefesseur que lui-meme. Il habita Saint-Petersbourg, Tagerwilen, Constance, Munich et Stuttgart." No citation given. Duplicated copy provided by Jody Feldtman Wright.

[290] Feldmann, Kaspar, von Glarus, geb. daselbst 1805, est kaufmann is Petersburg, spatter privatisierend in Tagerwilen, Konstanz und Munchen, malte autodidaktisch mit wachsendem Erfolge, Landschafen und Architekturen in aquarelle. Er starb 1866 in Stuttgart. N. Z. Ztg. v. 12 Dez. 1901, Bell. zu Nr. 344, Feuilleton. – Glarn. Nachr. 1901, Nr. 92. Ernst Bu---. Duplicated copy labeled: Neue Zurcher Zeitun, Pp. 450. Duplicated copy provided by Jody Feldtman Wright.

Tagerwilen, Konstanz and Munich, and that he was a growing success in (painting) landscape and architecture – he worked in watercolor.[291] One of his paintings, "Casino und Hauptstrasse" (Club on Main Street) painted in 1856-58, [292] can be seen in a book called "Glarus."[293]

At one point, Caspar gave 2 of his father's paintings to each of his children.[294] Many of these paintings have been retained in the family.[295]

***

What kernels of truth can be found in the family lore? Caspar's father was a "von Feldtmann," but it seems unlikely that there was a title to inherit. Caspar was not the first-born son, but he was the oldest living son in the von Feldmann family when he emigrated from Switzerland. Caspar's father was a painter and well-enough known to be included in a book on Glarus painters. Caspar's family was from Glarus so Caspar was probably born in Switzerland – not in Russia. Perhaps Caspar was born while his mother was away from home. However, there are enough references to a Russian family connection - especially through Caspar's mother - to say that Caspar's family did have family ties to "Russia." Did the "Feldmann" Family live in a "castle" near "Napoleon's brother?" Unlikely. However, it is likely that Caspar George Feldtmann did come to the United States for the opportunities the new country afforded. Those opportunities probably were the rewards promised to immigrants when they enlisted and served in the Union Army during the Civil War.[296]

---

[291] Translation thanks to JoAnn Seibert.

[292] "Casino an der Haupstrabe," 1856-1858, aquarelle, 60 x 47, Casino— Gesellschaft Hotel, Glarnerhof, Glarus, Switzerland. "This work is on display at the Hotel Glarnerhof in Glarus." Provided by Jody Feldtman Wright.

[293] Unpublished letter from Jody Feldtman Wright to Jack Feldtman, dated: 26 July 1985.

[294] Per Gail Fordyce to Barbara Hunter on Gail's visit to Oregon.

[295] Upon his father's death, Bob Engelhardt, who was the executor of his father's estate, took the paintings given to Sophie Feldtman Engelhardt to either the De Young Museum or The Palace of the Legion of Honor (both San Francisco fine art museums) and was told either that the paintings were not originals or that they were not very valuable. Helen Engelhardt Hunter: story as told to Barbara Hunter.

[296] That might have been the same for Caspar's younger brother, Heinrich

It appears that there are many kernels of truth in the family lore. There also seems no doubt that Bob's grandfather, Caspar Georg Feldtmann, was an adventurous, colorful fellow and a good story teller as his stories were passed down in the Feldtmann family for generations.

***

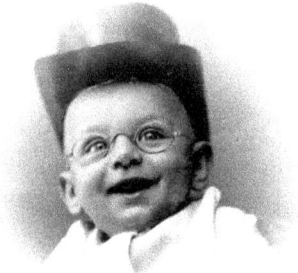

On May 1, 1896, Alex and Sophie's first child, Oswald Kaspar Engelhardt, was born at the Feldtmann Family home, 420 Garden Street, San Antonio.[297]

***

Late in 1890's, there were difficulties in the Caspar and Anna Feldtmann marriage. At one point, Caspar George is said to have left for San Francisco, and, that when he had returned home, his business partner had cheated him out of his share of the business.[298] In his papers at the Veteran's Home of California, Caspar Georg says that he was divorced from his wife, Anna.[299] [300]

Alexander Wilhelm Feldmann, who also came to New York and married. Unfortunately, Heinrich was only about 20 when he died.

[297] There were no Texas birth certificates issued at the time. But Oswald's birth is attested to in a letter by attending doctor, Dr. S. Berg of San Antonio Texas. This letter was provided when Oswald applied for Seaman's Protection in 1918. "Applications for Seaman's Protection Certificates, 1916-1940." *Ancestry.com* database entry for Oswald Engelhardt.

[298] Conversation with Sandra Fahnert Stacy.

[299] Previously cited. Letter summarizing records from the Veterans Home of California.

Whether these difficulties encouraged the Engelhardts to move is uncertain, but the Feldtmann home on Garden Avenue must have become an increasingly challenging place to live and to raise a child. By about 1898, the Engelhardt's had moved to San Francisco.[301] Alex was working as a watchmaker. Robert Caspar Engelhardt was born a little over 2 years later, on December 28, 1900 - just 3 days after Christmas.

Oswald and Robert Engelhardt in San Francisco, California.

---

[300] "Real Estate Transactions." (Notice of a property transfer) *San Antonio Light*, Vol. 21, Nos 108, 7 May 1902. "C. G. Feldtmann to Anna Feldtmann 75 x 155 feet, west side of Presa St., City, block 902. $500."

[301] By the time Alex and his family decided to head for San Francisco in 1898, the City would have literally glittered with opportunity: an affluent population which could purchase fine jewelry and watches; museums, theaters and an opera house which attracted world famous talent; and prominent German social societies, called "Verein," whose performances attracted city-wide attention. For Alex, who had performed on stage since he was a young boy and who continued to be an active member of the German singing societies, San Francisco certainly was a larger stage for Alex's fine musical talent.

8
THE ENGELHARDTS
SAN FRANCISCO

Bob Engelhardt was born in San Francisco and grew up in a very lively, talented German-American family - which seemed to enjoy the "finer things in life" - elegant homes, beautiful furnishings, excellent food, fine art and classical music.

The Engelhardts at Home. Helen, Sophie and Alex.

When you entered the Engelhardt home, many lovely things would catch your eye. Sophia' grandfather's pictures hung on the walls. There was a piano and a piano bench filled with musical scores - as well as a music cabinet whose shelves were filled with even more sheet music. A bronze statue of a smith crafting a piece of iron dominated a table top. Handcrafted glass bowls, carved ivory figures, and beautiful ceramic pieces complemented the décor.

The furniture was made of heavy, dark, imposing wood with curved arm rests. Two of the more decorative chairs had straight backs inlaid with wood and mother-of-pearl. There was a tea trolley on wheels that could be rolled out so tea could be served to guests. A large, wind-up phonograph played classical music - including operas sung by Caruso.[302] A tall, white French ceramic clock, decorated with painted roses, claimed the mantel.[303]

It seems fair to say that the Engelhardt home was formal and gracious - a place of comfort where the Engelhardts could entertain in style.

The Engelhardts entertaining in style. Alex Engelhardt is at the head of the table. Around 1900.

---

[302] The Engelhardt family's wind-up phonograph was in the basement of my mother's, Helen Engelhardt Hunter's, house on 30th Avenue in San Francisco. As a child, I would wind up the phonograph and listen to Caruso sing. The phonograph used a steel, or sometimes a bamboo, needle and played music at various speeds depending on how tightly the spring of the phonograph was wound. My mother always listened to opera on Sundays when I was young. Later, of course, she listened to the San Francisco Giants games. BLH

[303] My mother, Helen Engelhardt Hunter, inherited this furniture and many other decorative items from her parents so I am merely describing the family furniture that my mother retained for her own home. I can confirm from early photographs that this was the way the Engelhardt's home was furnished. BLH

Sophie was considered a wonderful cook.[304] The evidence for Sophie's cooking excellence was said to be that, when the "German Navy" came to San Francisco, the officers were always entertained by the Engelhardts.[305]

As a cook, Sophie seems to have produced a combination of German and Texas style dishes.[306] At Thanksgiving, for example, a vegetable succotash of green beans, okra and canned tomatoes was always served.[307] The day after Thanksgiving, left-over mashed potatoes were always turned into German potato pancakes which she called "kartoffelpuffers."[308] One added a little flour, salt, fried onions, and an egg to the mashed potatoes, mix everything thoroughly, and then fried small potato pancakes in butter - a recipe that I would highly recommend.

Another of Sophie's recipe that probably came straight from Texas was "Spanish Rice" made with bacon crumbles. I recall that the dish was made as follows:

Sophie's Spanish Rice

First fry a few slices of bacon.

Remove the bacon from the pan and fry chopped onions, celery and green peppers in the bacon grease.

---

[304] My mother, who I knew to be a great cook, always said that she was a good cook – but that she was nowhere as good a cook as her mother, Sophie. BLH

[305] Helen Hunter: story told many times to her daughter Barbara Hunter.

[306] I'm identifying my mother's favorite dishes which she must have learned to cook from her mother, Sophie Feldtmann Engelhardt.

[307] Verne Moller, an old family friend, would remark on this dish as something traditionally served by Sophia at Engelhardt dinners. Verne, good soul that he was, always praised the succotash highly. Even as a child, I thought Verne was a good sport about the succotash.

[308] My mother knew only very few German words. Although her parents spoke German among themselves, they did not speak German to their daughter as "they wanted her to be an American." My mother always regretted that she couldn't speak two languages. However, her parents always called her, "Schattzi" which means "little darling" in German.

After removing the excess grease, add cooked rice and chopped tomatoes, a little tomato sauce, (perhaps some Worcestershire Sauce), salt and chili powder to taste.

Crumble bacon and add.

Put the mixture in casserole dish. Put Mexican cheese on top.

Bake until hot. (30-45 minutes) Delicious.

The Engelhardt children were taught to eat and enjoy all sorts of food that we don't necessarily put on the table today. Sophie's daughter, Helen Engelhardt Hunter, for example, made a variety of dishes that she must have learned from her mother: liver and onions, tongue boiled in spices (love it), and tripe in tomato sauce (avoid it). When she could get brains from the butcher, Helen would scramble brains and eggs for breakfast and exclaim how delicious they were. After Helen roasted a piece of meat, she removed the bone marrow and spread it on toast with salt and pepper for a little treat. She had a good cut of meat specially ground by the butcher, and made it into "steak tartare"- raw hamburger with seasonings. She loved it but also fed some of it to her daughter telling her daughter how tasty it would be. It was! Steak tartare was also something Helen's father, Alex, especially liked.

With all this interesting, unusual food to eat, you naturally came to enjoy all sorts of well-prepared food. You were also taught that if you didn't like a particular dish, you never made a negative comment as you might spoil other peoples' "enjoyment" of their food.[309] Enjoyment of food was a key concept with the Engelhardts.

In those days, San Francisco was filled with wonderful French bakeries and marvelous delicatessens whose pungent, mouth-watering aromas tempted San Franciscans to sample the wares. Bob's father, Alex, would bring home a plate of delicacies – cheeses and sausage meats- for the family. Pungent Limburger cheese was a special favorite of Bob's. According to Sue Arden West, "...regarding Grandpa Bob – Mom says he LOVED limburger cheese – the stinkier the better."

***

---

[309] My mother wasn't angry when she said this, just a firm, no nonsense instruction as to how to approach the enjoyment of food- for yourself and for others.

Sue West also remembered her Grandpa Bob's sense of humor:

"…over the years I always heard how much Bob laughed & was joyous. Mom said she felt very loved by him. I have a wonderful memory of him on his hands & knees chasing me down the hall at Grandma's house. I do remember his happy eyes. Boy, wouldn't he be happy to hear us talking about that."

Bob Engelhardt might have gotten his well-known sense of fun from his father, Alexander Gustave Engelhardt, who was also said to have an up-beat personality.[310] For example, Verne Moller, a long-time family friend, described how Alex enjoyed performing "magic" tricks such as having his walking cane "stand by itself." Alex actually had a black string attached to either of his knees and when the cane was placed upright against the black thread, the cane magically appeared to stand on end- without touching anything.

In trying to describe her father's up-beat personality, Helen Engelhardt Hunter told a story of her father and the opening of the Golden Gate Bridge. That first day, May 27, 1937, the bridge was opened only to foot traffic. According to Helen, not only did her father, Alex, walk across the bridge on opening day, he managed to be one of the first (if not the very first) to do so.[311] Helen said that this example of his exuberant participation in events and activities was very typical of her father.[312]

Although Alex seemed to thrive in San Francisco's sophisticated atmosphere, Bob's mother, Sophia Feldtman Engelhardt, was a much more reserved personality.[313] She always seemed to long for her family in Texas,

---

[310] Verne Moller, a long-time family friend: stories told to Barbara Hunter.

[311] Helene Engelhardt Hunter: story told to her daughter, Barbara Hunter.

[312] Another example was that when the Engelhardt family visited the Carlsbad Caverns (or perhaps the Oregon Caves), visitors were told to stay with the guide or they could be lost in the caves – a very dangerous situation. Alex, entranced by the stalactites, wandered off and was lost for a while. Helen Engelhardt Hunter: story as told to Barbara Hunter.

[313] From my mother's stories, I would describe Sophia as a very nice person and a loving mother (as my mother really liked her), but Sophia was also fairly strict and rather "high strung." She was easily upset by changing circumstances to which she reacted strongly. My mother believed that this was at least partly a result of Sophia being in an "arranged marriage." BLH

for Texas itself, and for open country in general. Over her lifetime, Sophia made several trips back to Texas to be with her family. Even toward the end of her life, when Sophia was confined to bed with heart problems, she "rose up" and said, "I want to see Texas one more time." In order for Sophia to make this visit, Sophia's daughter Helen and Helen's husband, Louis Hunter, drove Sophie all the way to San Antonio – all 2000 miles - and back. Actually, Louis drove all the way because Helen quickly became hypnotized by the lines in the middle of the road, which began to double and wobble, and so could not share the task of driving.[314]

In describing her mother, Helen recalled a time when she was 16 and learning to drive. By then the Engelhardts were living in Los Altos. Helen and her mother had taken the family automobile to one of the fruit orchards so Helen could safely practice her driving. However, Helen's mother became so nervous and upset (although nothing really had happened) that Helen, also a nervous person, lost perspective and, instead of driving in straight line, drove round and round and round the trees in the orchard.[315] Years later, Helen, who also had a good sense of humor, thought this story was hysterical as she could still vividly picture the two of them zooming in rapid circles around the orchard.[316] [317]

***

---

[314] Helene Engelhardt Hunter: story as told to her daughter, Barbara Hunter.

[315] Helene Engelhardt Hunter: story as told to her daughter, Barbara Hunter. Years later, my mom, with her good sense of humor, thought this incident was very funny. It gave her a good laugh to tell this story. BLH

[316] Sophia had interesting concerns and oft repeated sayings. She said that a "lady never had rough elbows" and urged applying lotion to your elbows at every opportunity - which I still do to this day with any lotion left over from applying make-up. Sophia favorite saying was, "It is better to be rich than good looking, but it sure is hell to be cheated out of both."

[317] Helen Engelhardt Hunter: story as told to Barbara Hunter.

From a very young age, Bob knew his grandmother, Anna Albrecht Feldtmann, and the rest of his Texas family. That's because the Feldtmann family, despite long distances between them, always remained close.[318] For example, early in the 1900's, just a few years after Bob was born, Sophia took her two sons, Oswald and Bob, to San Antonio to visit the Feldtmann Family.

Bob now had many cousins whom he met at this "reunion." Bob's Aunt Lou Cahen had had 3 children: Camille, Edna and Carl.[319] His aunt, Annie Deussen, also had several children: George, Lucille, Anita and Frank. Aunt Mary had married Henry W. Rogers April 2, 1901 and had one child, Blanche.

Bob's Uncle Alex Feldtmann,[320] Uncle Earnest,[321] Uncle George,[322] Aunt Katie[323] and Uncle Oscar Feldtmann were not married at the time of the visit. Uncle Oscar never married.

---

[318] There are stories and pictures of numerous family reunions, get-togethers and vacations, and tales of the continuous support provided by one family member to another. There was constant interaction and communication between members of the family – including letters and visits between the Feldtmann family in California and the family in San Antonio.

[319] Bob would eventually have one more Cahen cousin - Isabelle.

[320] Alex Feldtman married twice. In 1899, he married Della Fulton. They were divorced 6 months later. Then on May 5th, 1909, Alex married Marie Cecile Cotaya. There were no children from either marriage. In: "225560, Estate of Caspar G. Feldtmann, Dec'd. Proof of Heirship; Annie Feldtmann, et al." State of Texas, Bexar County. (Filed: January 17, 1928)

[321] Bob's Uncle Earnest, who was 16 in 1900, moved back to San Antonio-seemingly right after Bob's birth in December of 1900. He had returned to San Antonio in 1901. He was working as a clerk and living at the family home at 420 Garden Avenue.

[322] In 1917, Bob's Uncle George married Ella Lee Bean. They had five children: Katherine Louise, Earnest Floyd, Ellen "Fern," George, Jr., and Eldon Warren Feldtman. (Note: Marriage date from notes of Fern Fahnert Feldtman.)

[323] On May 27, 1907, Katherine Louise Feldtman, Bob's Aunt Katie, married George Hudson Hicks. They had one daughter, Vivian, on December 10, 1921.

The Feldtmann family as they are related to Bob Engelhardt:[324]

1. Aunt Louisa "Lou" Feldtmann Cahen
2. Bob's Mother, Sophia Feldtmann Engelhardt
3. Uncle Ernest Feldtmann
4. Uncle George Caspar Feldtmann
5. Aunt Katherine Louise "Katie" Feldtmann Hicks
6. Cousin Camille "Millie" Cahen (b. 23 Feb 1891)
7. Cousin George Deussen (b. 6 Apr 1895)
8. Cousin Edna Cahen (b. 30 May 1896)
9. Cousin Carl Cahen (b. 9 Oct 1903)
10. Aunt Annie Feldtmann Deussen
11. Brother Oswald Kaspar Engelhardt (b. 1 May 1896)
12. **Robert Caspar Engelhardt (b. 28 Dec 1900)**
13. Grandmother Anna Albrecht Feldtmann
14. Cousin Blanch Rogers (b. 29 Jan 1903)
15. Aunt Mary Feldtmann Rogers
16. Cousin Lucille Deussen (b. 13 May 1898)
17. Cousin Anita "Bunny" Deussen (b. 15 Jul 1899)
18. Cousin Frank Deussen (b. 12 Jul 1905)

---

[324] The "reunion" was probably early 1906 – sometime after the death of Caspar George Feldtmann who died on the 18th of January, 1906. (Photograph with permission of Katy Feldtman.)

Not pictured are Uncle Alexander Feldtmann and Uncle Oscar Feldtmann.

***

Bob also must have known his Texas grandfather, Caspar George Feldtmann. From April 4, 1904 until his death on January 19, 1906, Bob's grandfather lived at the Veterans' Home of California in Yountville, which is north of San Francisco. The Veterans' Home, as it still does today, provided housing and care to older or disabled veterans. As a veteran of the Civil War (Union Army) and having heart problems, Caspar Feldtman qualified to be there.

The Veterans' Home was situated in very pleasant surroundings, but it had a military atmosphere. The barracks, which housed about 800 disabled war veterans, were large wooden Victorian structures. The spacious grounds were landscaped and the whole establishment was set in a valley surrounded by picturesque hills.

Although the Veteran's home seemed a very congenial place to live (especially for the time period), Caspar Feldtmann probably chose to live at the Veterans' Home of California because it was a facility that accepted Union Army Civil War veterans, and it was a facility which was close to his daughter, Sophie.

On 18th of January, 1906, after a stay of 2 ½ years at the Veterans Home of California in Yountville, Bob's grandfather, Caspar George Feldtmann, passed away and was buried in the cemetery at the veterans' home.[325]

***

Just 3 months later, on April 18, 1906, San Francisco was devastated by the earthquake and fire. Bob's family was living just north of San Francisco, in San Rafael, California, when the catastrophic 1906 earthquake occurred.

Helen, who was not even born at the time of the earthquake, always said that she was told that her family home survived the earthquake and that the Engelhardts were relieved and grateful not to have to camp out in "the park."[326] Helen assumed that her mother meant her family was in San Francisco during the quake and that they were glad not to join the over 200,000 San Franciscans that took up temporary residence in Golden Gate Park.

Helen also "knew" that her family had gone to San Raphael and that her

---

[325] Caspar Georg Feldtmann's grave: Yountville, California, The Veterans Home of California, Cemetery, Section A, Row 9, Grave 26.

[326] Story from Sophia Engelhardt to her daughter, Helen – Helen Engelhardt Hunter as retold to Barbara Hunter.

family remained there while San Francisco was being rebuilt. And, she "knew" that her father, Alex, continued to work in San Francisco by taking the ferry from Marin County (from Sausalito, or perhaps from Tiburon) to the Ferry Building at the end of Market Street in San Francisco.

But, according to the San Raphael City Directory, the Engelhardts were living in San Raphael by 1905.[327] They continued to live there until 1908.

This move to San Raphael in Marin County from San Francisco seemed to make sense on at least two levels. One, the Engelhardts, especially Sophie, always seemed to love the less developed, more scenic regions of Marin County. And, two, San Raphael was much closer to Sophia's father, Caspar George Feldtmann, who was living in Yountville.

Sophia Feldtmann Engelhardt
with her two sons, Oswald and Robert

---

[327] "San Raphael California, City Directory, 1905." *Ancestry.com* database entry for Alex Engelhardt.

Once in San Raphael, Alex had an easy commute on the ferry to San Francisco. Harold Gilliam's book, "San Francisco Bay," provides a vivid description of the "twice daily social period" provided by the commuters' ferry ride. The passenger ferries were "floating clubhouses" whose regular members caught the same ferry ride each day and formed "well-defined in-groups-" each with its own customs. The ferry ride was described as an enjoyable time – sometimes music was provided by a commuter chorus or by a crew member who liked to sing opera.[328] Alex would have loved it.

Although the Engelhardts were living in San Raphael in 1906, they did experience the full force of the earthquake. That's because the 1906 quake devastated a "swath twenty to forty miles wide, running 200 miles from Fort Bragg in the north to Salinas in the south…"[329] This whole area was hit as hard or harder than San Francisco. For example, Santa Rosa, in Marin County, "was a nightmare scene - every brick building in town was down."[330]

If the Engelhardts had driven to Sausalito in the very early the next morning after the quake, they would have been able to see the light from several of the major San Francisco fires reflected. "off the waters of the Golden Gate."[331]

After the quake, the fires raged in San Francisco, the water gave out, the dynamiting to establish fire lines began - and 3 days later much of old San Francisco was in ruins. But, the ferries kept running. The Ferry Building at the foot of Market Street was untouched by the fires, and the ferries continued to run - on schedule – throughout the fires and the blasting - and, later, throughout the reconstruction of the City.

Like George Nimmo, Bob's father, Alexander Gustave Engelhardt, probably benefitted from the dislocation caused by the earthquake and the rebuilding of the City. It apparently allowed Alex to start his own business. In 1907, a year after the earthquake, Alex was listed in the city directory as a "retail jeweler" at 443 Van Ness Avenue.[332] A year after that, his jewelry

---

[328] Gilliam, Harold. *San Francisco Bay*. Garden City, New York: Doubleday & Company, Inc., 1957, Pp. 127-129.

[329] Bronson, William. *The Earth Shook – The Sky Burned*. Garden City, New York: Doubleday & Company Inc., 1959. Pp. 29.

[330] Ibid. Bronson, Pp. 29.

[331] Ibid. Bronson, Pp. 68.

[332] "U.S. City Directories, 1822-1995. "(San Francisco, California, City Directory 1907) *Ancestry.com* database entry for Alex Engelhardt.

business was located at 22 Montgomery Street - a prestigious location right off Market Street, the commercial center of San Francisco's Downtown.[333]

Alex also advertised that he bought and sold silver and gold, which, in the aftermath of the quake, would have been a welcome service that was required during those tough times.[334] [335]

In 1909 the Engelhardt family returned to San Francisco where they had an apartment at 668 Hyde, (Post St. and Hyde St.) - just a 9-block walk to Alex's store on Montgomery Street and less than a block from where they had lived just before they went to San Raphael.

After the open spaces of Marin County, an apartment near downtown might not have suited the family, because a year later, in 1910, the Engelhardts rented a home at 133 Baker Street.[336] The Engelhardt's Baker Street home was a ½ block from the Panhandle of Golden Gate Park. It was also just 2 blocks from the Haight Street shopping area which bordered Buena Vista Park.

That meant the Engelhardt home on Baker Street was just a few blocks away from the Nimmo's home on Buena Vista Avenue. In 1910, Bob would have been 9 and Rose 7 years old. Early in their lives, they might have met at school or when their mothers went shopping on Haight Street.

The Engelhardts only lived on Baker Street for a couple of years. In 1913, the Engelhardts moved to 721 Arguello Blvd.[337] just two blocks from the Arguello Entrance to Golden Gate Park. They were in a lovely

---

[333] "U.S. City Directories, 1822-1995." (San Francisco, California, City Directory, 1908) *Ancestry.com* database entry for Alex Engelhardt.

[334] "Cash for Old Gold and Silver – Precious Gem Stones." *San Francisco Call*, 19 Sept 1908 – Sat. page 12. *Newspapers.com* database entry for Alex Engelhardt.

[335] Alex also got himself into a bit of trouble over this buying and selling silver and gold as an employee of the United States Mint (San Francisco) sold him some gold- right from the mint -and Alex had to prove that he actually didn't know that the gold he bought came from the U. S. Mint.

[336] In the census, this address looks like it is for a home, but the address could have been for a flat or apartment. "1910 United States Federal Census." *Ancestry.com* database entry for Alex Engelhardt.

[337] "U.S. City Directories, 1822-1995." (San Francisco, California, City Directory 1911) *Ancestry.com* database entry for Alex Engelhardt.

Victorian home[338] whose location made a walk thought the vast Golden Gate park almost mandatory.

Bob would have been 12 or 13 when the Engelhardt moved to Arguello. Bob's brother, Oswald, who would have been about 17, left home and went to sea.[339] Oswald's 1918 "Application for a Seaman's Protection Certificate" says that he went to sea in 1913, worked as an "oiler" and that he, "arrived at the port of San Francisco on May 30, 1916 on the "Str. Minnesota" on which vessel he worked as oiler …."

Helen Engelhardt Hunter said her brother had been "around the world."[340] Oswald's three years at sea, starting when he was 17, makes this family story very likely. Oswald never is listed as an "oiler" in the San Francisco City Directory. Instead, in the 1914, 1915, and 1918 city directories, Alex is listed as a "painter."[341] It seems that Oswald might have gone to sea and worked as an "oiler" to support his real desire to become an artist.

Oswald, who was probably trained by his father, was also a watchmaker. In 1916, he was living in San Antonio with his Aunt Katie at 231 Essex Ave in San Antonio and working as a watchmaker at Bell Jewelry Company. In 1917, he was back in San Francisco and working as a decorator at A. C. Walker and Company.[342] So it seems that while Bob was in his late teens, his older brother, Oswald, was essentially out and about and trying to make his way in the world.

***

---

[338] This "home" is now replaced by a large apartment house, so the "lovely Victorian home" is surmised from the surrounding lovely Victorian homes that still grace the neighborhood.

[339] "Applications for Seaman's Protection Certificates, 1916-1940." (Records of the Bureau of Marine Inspection and Navigation; Record Group Number: 41; Box Number: 031 - San Francisco) *Ancestry.com* database entry for Oswald Engelhardt.

[340] Helen Engelhardt Hunter: story as told to her daughter, Barbara Hunter.

[341] Alex is an artist, a "painter." U.S. City Directories, 1822-1995." (San Francisco, California, City Directory 1914, 1915, 1918) *Ancestry.com* database entry for Oswald Engelhardt.

[342] "U.S. City Directories, 1822-1995." (San Francisco, California, City Directory 1917) *Ancestry.com* database entry for Oswald Engelhardt.

However, by 1914, Bob's Uncle Ernest[343] had moved back in with the Engelhardts.[344] Ernest, at 29, was still unmarried. He had not lived with the Engelhardts since he returned to Texas in 1901. For 8 to 9 years, Ernest generally worked as a plumber in Texas and had lived with his family at 420 Garden Street.

In 1909, Anna Albrecht Feldtman, who must have been ill by that time, lived at 515 Presa with her sons, Ernest and George. In 1910, Anna lived with her daughter, Katie, and Katie's husband, George Hicks. George Hick's sister, Kate Garlock, also lived there. Kate Garlock was a trained nurse at the hospital and probably helped care for Anna. Anna Albrecht Feldtmann died on the 17th of May 1910.[345]

It appears that Ernest might have left Texas upon the death of his mother, Anna Albrecht Feldtmann because Ernest is not found in the San Antonio City Directories after 1910. Since Ernest was always close to his sister, Sophia, he might have headed for California after his mother's death. But his movements from 1910 to 1914 aren't clear. Ernest seems only to have joined the Engelhardt family in San Francisco in 1914.

By 1914, Ernest was a "motorman" for the San Francisco Municipal Railway.[346] He worked some of the time on the famous San Francisco cable cars.[347] He kept his "motorman" job with the City for the rest of his working career.[348]

Ernest lived with the Engelhardts until about 1918 when he married Margaret Mary Turel (Bob's Aunt Marguerite). Bob's Uncle Ernest and

---

[343] Earnest had dropped the "a" in his name and now called himself "Ernest."

[344] "U.S. City Directories, 1822-1995." (San Francisco, California, City Directory 1914) *Ancestry.com* database entry for Ernest Feldtman.

[345] Also dying a little more than a year after Anna who died on May 17, 1910 was her son, Alexander Feldtmann (2 Nov 1911). His wife, Maria Cecile Cotaya Feldtmann, died (28 Mar 1910) just 2 months before Anna Feldtmann died.

[346] "California, Voter Registrations. 1900-1968 for Ernest Feldtmann." (San Francisco County, 1914) *Ancestry.com* database entry for Ernest Feldtmann.

[347] Family story recalled by Barbara Hunter.

[348] "U.S. City Directories, 1822-1995." (San Francisco, California, City Directory, all available years after 1914) *Ancestry.com* database entry for Ernest Feldtmann.

Aunt Marguerite made their home on Divisadero Street.[349]

Marguerite was a convent raised child of French immigrant parents. The family story is that Marguerite, who was born in California in November of 1886,[350] quickly became an orphan when her French immigrant parents died of the flu. Her godparents[351] placed Marguerite in an orphanage. Marguerite was raised by nuns at the Notre Dame Institute, Orphan Asylum, in San Jose, California. By 1910, she was a maid with a San Jose family.

When she married Ernest in 1918, Marguerite was 32, Ernest Feldtman was 34. On the 8th of July, 1922, they had their first, and only, child, John Caspar Feldtman. Everyone always called him "Jack."

Jack Feldtman, Alex Engelhardt and Ernest Feldtman. San Francisco. About 1938. Possession of Barbara Hunter.

---

[349] Apartments at 1411 Divisadero (1918-1924) and 1336 Divisadero (1925) In: "U.S. City Directories, 1822-1995." (San Francisco, California, City Directory, 1918-1925) *Ancestry.com* database entry for Ernest Feldtman.

[350] Most United States Federal Census information shows Marguerite as 2 years younger than Ernest which would make her birth year 1888. However, the 1910 United States Federal Census says that Marguerite was 13 and born in November of 1886. When women's ages change over time, I usually opt for the age on the documentation when they were very young - that is, before they give the information themselves.

[351] I saw these godparents years later when they showed up to visit Aunt Marguerite. Shirley Gomez Feldtman, Aunt Marguerite's daughter-in-law, told me that they were rich, that they had once owned the land on which San Francisco's Union Square was located in downtown San Francisco, but that Marguerite never received any money from them.

***

On the 5th of January 1916, the Engelhardt family had a daughter, Helen Elsie Engelhardt. She was born at home, at 721 Arguello Blvd. Given that she was about 15 years younger than her brother Bob, she always described herself as "an afterthought." Bob loved his sister dearly. They loved and supported each other all their lives.[352]

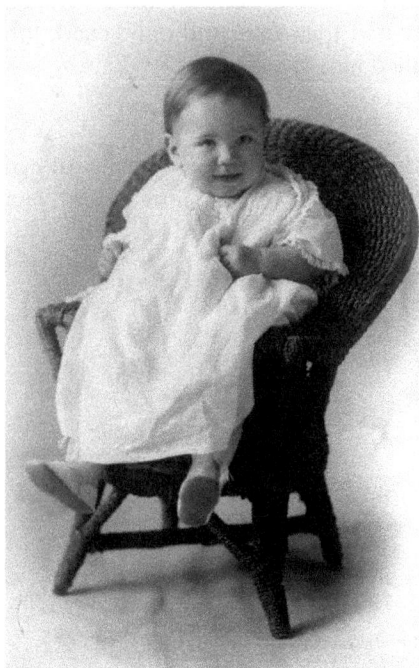

Helen Elsie Engelhardt. Photograph in possession of Barbara Hunter.

***

As opposed to Rose Nimmo and her family who lived in their cozy home on Buena Vista, the Engelhardts moved every few years. Between the time he was born until he was 18, Bob lived in 7 homes:[353]

---

[352] Helen Elsie Engelhardt Hunter was always called "Helene." The name was given to her by her brother, Bob. He didn't think that "Helen" was sophisticated enough for her and decided she should be called "Helene." The name stuck. My mother loved it and was never known by anything else. In fact, "Helene Hunter" is the name on her grave as "Helene" was who she was.

[353] After 1920, the Engelhardts lived several more places: 947 Noe Street., San Francisco, CA from 1920 – 1928; Los Altos, CA from 1930 - 1933/4; 626 – 17th Ave., San Francisco, CA in 1934; and 115 – 12th Ave., San Francisco, CA in 1938-1942.

3 Post Ct, SF, CA	1900 - 1901
705 Hyde, SF, CA	1901 - 1905
San Rafael, Marin, CA	1905 - 1908
668 Hyde, SF, CA	1908 - 1909
133 Baker Street, SF, CA	1909 - 1912
721 Arguello Blvd., SF, CA	1913 - 1917
1104 Noe St., SF, CA	1918 - 1919/20

The Engelhardts also bought a rustic vacation cabin in the hills above the little town of Glen Ellen. This vacation retreat was called "Waldruhe," which meant "Peaceful Woods."[354] The cabin was a single story wooden structure - 8 feet wide and 20 feet long (inside) - with a front porch and a back porch. From the back porch you overlooked the Valley of the Moon. The cabin was very primitive by today's standards, but it was typical of family vacation cabins of the time.

For many years, all the family enjoyed going to Waldruhe. The family could hike down to the "river to swim." Despite money troubles after the Depression, Sophie continued to hold on to Waldruhe. Waldruhe appears to have been in Sophie's name until she died on the 19th of March 1942.[355] The "Peaceful Woods" was her property and her treasured sanctuary- to the end.

---

[354] "Waldruhe Heights" is in Marin County, California. It is just up the mountain from the town of Glen Ellen. My mother's recollection was that they were able to hike down the mountain and go swimming in the river.

[355] "Enterprise School District: Waldruhe Heights Engelhardt. Sophia Engelhardt – Lot 4 Blk 16 Tp 6 R 6 Total ...$7.38. Engelhardt Sophia – Lot 3 Blk 16 Tp 6 R 6 Total.....$2.43." (newspaper notice) *The Press Democrat* (Santa Rosa, California), Tue. Jun 2, 1942. Pp. 7. In: *Newspapers.com* database entry for Sophia Engelhardt.

Bob and Sophie Engelhardt and "Kittie"[356] at Waldrurhe
(Peaceful Woods).
***

Life in San Francisco, with all the moves to new homes every few years, might have been a little chaotic for the Engelhardts, but it seems that it was interesting and pleasant - up to 1918.

World War I changed everything. Since 1914, Europe had been at war. But, it wasn't until April 6, 1917 that the United States became a participant. Two months later, June 5th of 1917, Oswald Engelhardt registered for the draft. His number was 258. It was, unfortunately, the first draft number selected. Oswald was one of first men drafted by the United States in World War I.[357] Oswald became a private in Company D, 361st Infantry, 91st Division of the United States Army. He trained at Fort Lewis, Washington.
***

On May 25, 1918, just before he left for Fort Lewis, Oswald married "Hannah," a Norwegian immigrant who was 4 years older than himself.[358]

---

[356] On the back of a picture in the same series is written, "Katchen is working hard." (sweeping) "Katchen is "little cat" or kitten. Sophia had a "Cousin Kittie" whose letter has been retained by Barbara Hunter. Therefore, I presume the little girl in the picture is Sophia's cousin, Kittie. Sophia also has a niece named "Alia." Nothing more is known of either person.

[357] "S.F.'s First 1917 Draftees." (newspaper article) *San Francisco Chronicle*, September 22, 1940. Page: 64. *Genealogybank.com* database entry for Oswald Engelhardt.

[358] I met Hannah many years later when she came to check on my mother after my father died in 1958. She was a tiny "German" lady that my mother instantly

He wrote her the following from Cambray Wood's, France on September 25th, 1918:[359]

"My dear Hanna;

In all the letters I have written to you, it has been impossible to tell you of our location. But now that we are just two kelometer's (sic) behind the front line trenches, I would like to write you a few lines, which if they are the last, I hope will reach you, through the kindness of some brother soldier that may chance to find them on my person together with the photographs of you and the folks. When we left New York our destination was Glasgow, Scotland, at which place we arrived July 18, 1918 after a 12 day voyage. From Glascow (Glasgow) we went by rail to South Hampton England, from there to Havor (sic), France. From Havor we made a two day trip across country to a little village named Epinant (sic). Epinant is about a five mile walk from the railway station. At the little village we stayed until Aug 20, and is the place which I received most of your dear letters. We made many a hike to nearby villages some of which are Sarrey, Martigny, Chaufort, Esine, Vacines and many other's all of which I do not remember. From Epinant we made a long hike to a station which name I do not remember, piled into a box car and started on our way to Demange. All our travels through France were made in box cars, 32 to 40 men together with their equipment in one small car. From Demange all our movements have been by night so I have never been able to get any names of villages from there on. Never the less after many nights of hiking, sleeping in the woods, grave yards, blown up churches and buildings, we find ourselves on the front, in the Verdun sector on the 25th day of September ready to take part at a moment's notice in what is supposed to be one of the strongest offensives ever known in this war. (break in the writing)

Sweetheart, Five day's have past since I discontinued writing and finds me with the rest of my brother soldiers on the battle front. Two days ago after battling with the Jerry we succeeded in driving them from the woods into the open country. Ever since that time we have lain in holes just large enough for one or two men. I and a friend dig together to keep warm with shrapnel bursting all around us. Even as I

---

recognized. My mother rushed forward to hug her. After "checking on us," she left. I never saw her again.

[359] Oswald's original letter is crammed on to a single sheet of 6" by 9" letter paper. It was obviously written during difficult times. I have retained most of Oswald's original spelling, grammar and spacing. It was never finished.

write I am ducking into my hole where my partner is fast asleep.

Hanna, my sweetheart, you may think it impossible to sleep with shells bursting around you, but, dear, after the last three nights of misery that we have gone through, three nights and three days of rain and ice cold weather always soaked to the bone, one sleeps through anything. This morning brought with it the first sunshine and it surely a God sent (sic) to us. Hanna girl, since the day I left you and my dear parents, brother and dear little sister standing at the Oakland station, I have said my prayers oftener than I did all in my life. The nearer the front we get the oftener I said them until "Our God in Heaven" finds me saying them and asking selfishly many, many things- every moment I have time enough to put my hands together and talk to him. I say to you, like I have said many, many times in my prayers, that if the "God All Mighty" wills my safe return to you, my dear wife, and my beloved parents, that I am going to be one of his most earnest followers and worshipers. I'll tell them how good our "God" was to me, and bring to him all of those that will lissen (sic) to me in my efforts......"[360] [361]

On the 9th of October, Oswald, who along with two or three others volunteered clear an area of snipers, was shot by a sniper and died instantly.[362] [363] Oswald was buried in France along with his brother soldiers.

The Engelhardt family was beyond grief at Oswald's death. It changed

---

[360] I typed the letter as it is – "spell check" continued to make some corrections - as I felt that this one letter, which is still in my possession, gives a good insight into the kind of man that Oswald was and shows the loving relationships in the Engelhardt family at this time.

[361] "Letter from Oswald Engelhardt "To My Dear Wife, Mrs. O. Engelhardt." Cambray Woods, France; Sept, 25, 1918. Possession of Oswald Engelhardt's niece, Barbara Hunter.

[362] Complete first-hand information on the battle in which Oswald was killed can be found in: "Red Cross Worker Tells Story of How Ninety-First Men Died on the Field of Action While Stopping (the) Enemy." (newspaper article) *Oregonian*, October 3, 1926. Page 71, 77. *genealogybank.com database* entry for Oswald Engelhardt.

[363] "The First Thirteen – Death of 1918 War Hero Provides Moral for 1940." (newspaper article) *San Francisco Chronicle*, Wednesday, September 18, 1940. Page 7.

them. Grieving became a focus of the family for several years. Helen Engelhardt Hunter was of the opinion that her mother, who was always high strung, never fully recovered.

In 1919 – 1920, the Engelhardts moved to 947 Noe Street. Hannah, who had lived with the Engelhardts since her marriage to Oswald, continued to live with the Engelhardts until about 1921.

On April 22, 1921, Hannah Engelhardt departed from New York on the Stavangerfjord for Bergen, Norway to attend to "family business."[364]

Also in 1921, the Engelhardt family had Oswald's body brought home from France. An announcement[365] in a 1921 San Francisco Chronicle said there was to be a funeral service for Oswald Engelhardt on October 22nd. Friends were invited to attend.

Oswald final resting place is the Engelhardt family plot in Cypress Lawn Memorial Park, Colma, California.[366]

Hannah arrived back in New York on October 24, 1922.[367] She came back to San Francisco and went on to make another life for herself. She was 30 years old.

Sophie Engelhardt (center) with her son, Bob, her daughter, Helen and her daughter-in-law, Hannah. San Francisco. About 1920. Photograph in possession of Barbara Hunter.

---

[364] "U. S. Passport Application, 1795-1925." *Ancestry.com* database entry for Hannah Engelhardt.

[365] "Death Notice." (newspaper notice) *San Francisco Chronicle*, 1921 –10- 21. Page 6. *genealogybank.com* database entry for Oswald Engelhardt.

[366] Cypress Lawn Memorial Park, Colma, California: Section K- Lot 203- Div. 3- South 1/2-#5. *Find A Grave* database entry for Oswald Engelhardt.

[367] "New York Passenger Lists, 1820-1957." (1922, Arrival: New York, New York) *Ancestry,.com* database entry for Hannah Engelhardt.

***

In 1918, at just 18, Bob found himself in a difficult situation: his parents were completely distraught and his little sister was just 2 years old. The family story is that Bob stepped-up to help raise his little sister, Helen. So, Bob stayed at home, and, at 18, he went to work.

In 1918, he was working as a clerk at Buckingham & Hecht, a shoe wholesaler on 1st Street in San Francisco. In 1920 he was in the U. S. Army working as a driver. By 1923 Bob was a customs "collector."[368]

Around 1924, Bob Engelhardt met Rose Nimmo – someone whose zest for life and sense of humor matched his own – someone with whom he could sing "Tea for Two" and mean every word!

---

[368] The 1923-25 San Francisco City Directories say Bob was a "collector." Right now, I cannot find where I read that he was a "customs" collector. In: "U.S. City Directories, 1822-1995." (San Francisco, California, City Directory 1923, 1924, 1925) *Ancestry.com* database entry for Robert Engelhardt. (Note: All his life, Bob was also a "collector" of United States postage stamps. He started me on my collections by generously giving me many duplicates from his collection.)

9
THE WEDDING - 1925

"Ahhhh – this is just so sweet to read! I can truly picture the whole thing & see Grandma Rose's smile. What a fun couple they were." – Beth Koller Whittenbury

***

Mr. and Mrs. George Nimmo
Request the honor of your presence at the
Marriage of their daughter
Rose Marion
To
Mr. Robert C. Engelhardt
On Wednesday evening, October the fourteenth
Nineteen hundred and twenty-five
At eight o'clock

All Saints Church
1350 Waller Street
San Francisco, California
***

On April 4, 1925, Robert Caspar Engelhardt and Rose Marion Nimmo became engaged. Bob was 23. Rose was 21. Rose, who seemed to enjoy writing, recorded many of the details of both her engagement and her wedding in her "Wedding Book." Additional details were found in Rose's copy of the "Solemnization of Matrimony."[369] [370] [371]

---

[369] Engelhardt, Rose Nimmo. *Wedding Book.* Unpublished journal. All details of the wedding recorded by Rose Marion Nimmo Engelhardt shortly after the

The Engagement.[372]

"Bob gave me my ring on the Saturday eve, April 4, 1925 while sitting on the Chesterfield in mother & dad's home. Was so thrilled over it that we drove over to Oakland & showed off. Went to grandmas,[373] & Tom's & Joe's."[374]

---

wedding. I made a few changes in the order of the narrative to let the story flow better and also made a very few spelling corrections. Otherwise, this chapter presents the wedding in Rose's words. The Wedding Book in possession of Rose's granddaughter, Beth Koller Whittenbury.

[370] The Form of Solemnization of Matrimony as contained in The Book of Common Prayer. Philadelphia: George M. Jacobs &Co., Publishers. (Note: This would be Rose's personal copy. The quotes in this book are from her handwritten entries.)

[371] All quotes in this chapter were taken directly from Rose's "Wedding Book," her "Solemnization of Matrimony" and her personal letters to Bob.

[372] Photograph: Rose Nimmo and Robert Engelhardt. In Rose Nimmo Engelhardt's photograph album. Titled: "The day we were engaged – April 4." Courtesy of Dolores Arden Engelhardt

[373] "Grandma" was Rosa Eichenberger Schnepple who now lived in Oakland with her unmarried sons who, of course, were Rose's uncles. At that time (1925), the married Schnepple sons also lived in Oakland, but not with their mother.

[374] "Tom & Joe" were Thomas Nimmo (Rose's brother) and Tom's wife, Josephine Louise Ferrero Nimmo, who were also living in Oakland at that time.

A small card anounced the "betrothal of Bob and Rose. Bob's sister, Helen Engelhardt Hunter, kept the betrothal card all her life.[375] [376]

Helen Engelhardt with Bob and Rose.

There were several parties in honor of the couple.

"Delightful surprise shower and party at Mother Engelhardt, September, 1925. A huge cake of pink frosting with two love birds on it made especially for us for the event."

"Joe Riegger[377] had a lovely dinner for us. Cake made with greetings for us. Fred Klein, Jo, Eve, Ed, Bob and I went to the theater following dinner."

"Lovely" dinner and shower at Mrs. Macmillan's home."[378]

The Wedding

Rose and Bob were married on October 14, 1925, at All Saints Episcopal Church[379] which is on Waller Street just off Masonic in the Height Ashbury

---

[375] Original in possession of Barbara Hunter.

[376] Photograph: Helen Engelhardt with Bob and Rose Engelhardt. San Francisco. 1926. Courtesy of Dolores Engelhardt Arden.

[377] Rose's best friend and maid of honor.

[378] Mrs. Jennie Sturtevant Macmillan was Rose's neighbor who lived next door at 489 Buena Vista Ave. She was the mother of Donald Macmillan who was one of the "Buena Vista Sextet."

[379] Both Rose and her mother, Lena Eichenberger Schnepple, were married in Episcopal churches – as was Claude Grant a member of the Sextet.

District of San Francisco. The Height Ashbury District is just down the hill from Buena Vista Heights where the Nimmos lived.

Founded in 1900, All Saints is a charming little church surrounded by the typically ornate San Francisco row houses. The church itself looks to be a modern version of English Tudor with a plaster and beam exterior.

"The alter of the church was decorated with palms and gladiolas...."

Center: Bob and Rose (Nimmo) Engelhardt.
Tom Nimmo is directly behind Rose.
Jack Ferrero is on the far left.
All Saints Episcopal Church, San Francisco.
October 14, 1925.
Courtesy of Dolores Engelhardt. Arden

Rose made a beautiful bride. In fact, the whole wedding party was quite elegant:

"My gown was white chiffon studded with rhinestones. Godets in the skirt made the dress very pretty. My Veil was tulle with scalloped edges and was held in place with a coronet of orange blossoms. I carried a shower bouquet of white cyclamen & lilies of the valley… with white streamers flowing from it."

"My Maid of Honor was my dearest chum Josephine Riegger who wore a gown of orchid georgette and silver. She wore a silver band in her hair and (?), silver slippers…. Jo Riegger's shower bouquet consisted of Ophelia (yellow and pink) roses from which fell a gold tulle ribbon."

"My two bridesmaids were Evelyn Ross whom I had paled with since the seven grade at school. She came all the way from Reedley, California to take part. She wore a green bouffant georgette dress trimmed with lace. She wore a wide silver band in her hair & silver hose and slippers……Evelyn carried a shower bouquet of baby roses that had an orchid tulle ribbon hanging from it."

"Gladyce Koch, whom I went around a good deal with at High School, and I had been a bridesmaid for her the past April wore a pale pink georgette gown trimmed with lace and also wore a silver band and silver (?)……Gladyce carried a shower bouquet of baby roses and had a green ribbon falling from it…"

The ushers all wore Tuxedos and wore white carnations in their lapels."

"Fred Klein, whom I had known through High School affairs sang beautifully, 'Oh Promise Me' and 'Because.' He was accompanied on the organ by Miss Cole who had taught me arithmetic in the eighth grade at Crocker Intermediate School. Gertie Levine, whom I had known since I was about 8 years old, also accompanied."

"The best man was my brother.[380] The ushers, Edwin Riegger, & Jack Ferrero."[381]

"Rev Pratt officiated at the Services in All Saints Church."

---

[380] Thomas Nimmo.

[381] John "Jack" Ferrero was the brother of Josephine Ferrero. Josephine was Tom Nimmo's wife. Jack's wife was Elaine Marie Pfortner, Hazel Pfortner's sister.

Rose's Thoughts on Her Wedding.

"I was the happiest girl on earth. As the day passed, I was thrilled, yet
with a little fear, wondering what would be the outcome of the step I
was about to take. At night when I started to dress, my heart was all a
flutter. Then when I put my veil on and the bridesmaids began to
come, then our flowers, I was shivering; but when I entered the
church and Fred had finished singing "Because" and "Oh Promise
Me", I felt at ease. When I stood with you before the crowd, at the
altar, with Rev. Pratt in front of us, I forgot the people, forgot
everything, but what he said to us. When he pronounced us Man and
Wife in the eyes of God and those friends, I knew then that I pledged
my love to you, and that as long as I live that I would love you
always."[382]

The Solemnization of Matrimony.[383]

On the flyleaf of "The Solemnization of Matrimony," Reverend Pratt
wrote:
    "With every hearty good wish
        For many long, happy and
            Successful years together
                In the mutual affection and trust of this
                    happy night.
    Schuyler Pratt
    October 14, 1925"

---

[382] Rose Nimmo Engelhardt's letter to Bob Engelhardt. October 14, 1926.

[383] The Form of Solemnization of Matrimony as contained in The Book of
Common Prayer. Philadelphia: George M. Jacobs &Co., Publishers.

This document was signed by 46 witnesses[384] to the wedding:

Josephine Riegger	Maid of Honor[385]
Thomas Nimmo	Best Man and brother of the bride
Evelyn Ross	Bridesmaid
Edwin Riegger	Usher
Gladyce Koch	Bridesmaid
Jack Ferrero	Usher
Fred Klein	Who sang "O Promise Me"
Mrs. Thomas Nimmo	Thomas Nimmo's wife, Josephine "Joe"
George O. Koch	Gladyce's Husband?
A. Engelhardt	Bob's father, Alexander Engelhardt
Sophia Engelhardt	Bob's mother
Mrs. George Nimmo	Rose's mother, Lena Schnepple Nimmo
George Nimmo	Rose's father
Adolph Gottschalk M.D.	
Minnie C. Gottschalk	
Thomar Emilie Rice	
E. Feldtman	Ernest Feldtman, Sophia Engelhardt's brother
J. G. Feldtman	Earnest's son, John Caspar Feldtman (?)
Mrs. E. Feldtman	Ernest's wife, Marguerite Turel Feldtman
Richard Schneider	
Mrs. H. Riegger	Josephine Riegger's mother (?)
Mrs. L. Mick	
L. F. Mick	
Norman Simmons	
Margaret Randall	
Frank Robinson	
Elaine Pfortner	Hazel Pfortner Schnepple younger sister
Ruth C. Neer	
Jack C Neer	
Arline Wright	
Hazel Schnepple	Hazel Pfortner Schnepple, Fred Schnepple's wife

---

[384] The signature these 46 people on this document (The Form of the Solemnization of Matrimony) emphasizes the importance of the "witness" role of wedding guests – something that we don't emphasize today. Only their signatures were written in this book.

[385] Descriptions of the witnesses was provided by me.

Grandma Schnepple   Rose's grandmother and Lena's mother, Rosa Eichenberger Schnepple

Dr. Brihard (sp?) Meyer

Jenny S. Macmillan (Mrs.) Jennie Sturtevant Macmillan, Donald Macmillan's mother and Rose's neighbor[386]

Donald G. Macmillan   Violet Nimmo Macmillan's husband, Jennie Sturtevant Macmillan's son

Violet Macmillan   Rose's cousin, daughter of Thomas Nimmo Jr. and Phoebe Neuman Nimmo

Thomas Nimmo   Rose's uncle, George Nimmo's brother

Mrs. Thomas Nimmo   Phoebe "Prock" Neuman Nimmo, Rose's aunt

Marion Hurlerant (sp?)

Frances Carson

J. W. George

Marion Haskell

Helen Marie Barry

Mary Ratliffe

Ellere (sp?) M. Bourke

---

[386] In the wedding book, Jennie S. Macmillan spells her name "Jenny."

The Reception.

The wedding reception consisted of a sit-down dinner for 65 people:[387]

> "…. which was held at Bob's home owing to there being more room. Dad & Mother hired Hubert's Catering Company to take full charge. A marvelous turkey dinner was served with the usual liquor for such affairs."

> "The flowers at the reception were pink and white. Where we were seated at the head was an immense heart made of palm leaves. Very, very pretty."

> "Many speeches were given for us. Two telegrams of congratulations had come from Detroit and Cleveland and were read to us by Don Macmillan.[388] While at the table I wore my veil. When the dancing started I took it off. I through (sic) my bouquet and Eve and Jo caught it amongst much fighting." [389]

---

[387] Since there were 46 witnesses and 65 people at the reception dinner, I assume that at least some of the 19 people who were not listed as witnesses were children. For example, Helen Engelhardt, Bob's sister, was not a witness- but she had to have been included in the wedding and reception. There are some adults which we know were in the wedding that didn't sign the book, e.g. Miss Cole and Gertie Levine. I expect some of the Schnepple uncles were there too- but did not sign the document.

[388] Donald George Macmillan who had been Rose's neighbor at 489 Buena Vista, a member of the Buena Vista Sextet and also the husband of Rose's cousin, Violet Nimmo.

[389] These telegrams would have been from Rose's father's family, the Nimmos, most of whom were still living back east.

The Nimmos that still lived in Detroit and might have sent the "telegram of congratulations" would have been Rose's grandmother, Marion Kerr Chalmers Nimmo, Rose's aunts: Mary Nimmo Scott and Marion Chalmers Nimmo, and Rose's uncle, Alexander Hughey Nimmo. Rose's grandfather, Thomas Nimmo, had died in 1903.

Rose's Aunt Jean D. Nimmo Alexander was living with her family in Cleveland,

"The wedding cake was a fruit cake, 3 tiers high covered with white frosting. On the top tier stood a miniature bride & groom. This was not cut at the reception but pieces were sent later. The bride's cake was pink frosting. The cake contained different articles, as thimbles, coins, etc. The table was beautifully decorated with streamers, flowers, etc."

Wedding Gifts.[390]

Ernest & Margaret[391]	Bridge Lamp
Mother, Dad and Helen Engelhardt[392]	Mantle Clock
Aunt Marion and Grandma[393]	12 silver teaspoons,
	6 salad forks,
	sugar spoon, butter knife
Uncle Dave and Aunt Lottie[394]	Sterling steak set
Uncle Alex and Aunt Mertie[395]	6 sterling knives, 6 forks,
	2 serving spoons

Ohio. She and her family would have sent the telegram from Cleveland.

Rose's Uncle David Nimmo had recently married in Toronto, Canada and, in 1925, still lived there with his wife.

Rose's Uncle Thomas Nimmo Jr. was living with his wife in Los Angeles, California. He and his family attended the wedding.

[390] This is a partial list of gifts, but all the Nimmo and Engelhardt family whose gifts were listed in the "Wedding Book" are listed here in this book. I'm sure there were more gifts.

[391] Ernest and Marguerite Feldtman, Bob's aunt and uncle.

[392] Sophia, Alex, and Helen Engelhardt.

[393] Aunt Marion Chalmers Nimmo and her mother, Marion Kerr Chalmers Nimmo, Rose's aunt and grandmother who were living in Detroit.

[394] David Nimmo and his wife Charlotte. Rose's aunt and uncle who were living in Toronto.

[395] Uncle Alexander Hughey Nimmo and his wife, Mertie McCloe Nimmo. They are Rose's aunt and uncle who were living in Detroit.

Sadie Burgess[396]	Sterling gravy ladle
Aunt Mary Scott[397]	Pillow cases & scarf
Aunt Marion[398]	Towels, 6 linen tea towels, embroidered guest towels, oven holder
Mother & Dad Nimmo[399]	Tea Wagon, Dining Room set, 10.00 Gold pieces
Bobby Dear	beautiful mother of pearl & amber dresser set

Rose's Trousseau
Black Satin Going away Dress
Tan Satin Dress
Printed Crepe Dress
Brown jersey suit
Black satin street dress with blue
Black velvet hat
Black satin and metal turban
Green georgette evening dress
1 pr. black satin slippers
1 pr. of black velvet slippers
Sport coat
6 teddies silk
4 silk gowns
3 silk bandeaus
6 pr. Silk hose
4 pr. Silk bloomers
4 silk nests
2 pr. pajamas
1 beautiful (?) teddie
1 white shirt
1 white satin (?)
1 white crepe slip

---

[396] A dear friend of Rose's aunt, Marion Chalmers Nimmo.

[397] Aunt Mary Nimmo Scott, Rose's aunt who was living in Cleveland, Ohio.

[398] This is probably Aunt Marion Chalmers Nimmo.

[399] Rose's parents: George and Lena Nimmo.

The Get-a-way.

Bob and Rose's "Get-a-way" was reported by Rose with such delight and relish that we can all be right there in the car with them as they sped around San Francisco escaping from their would-be kidnappers:

> "We made our get a way shortly after twelve. As I ran to jump into our limousine, George K grapped (sic) me, Bob ran & punched him, grabbed me and pushed me into the car. George ran to his car. Tom, the driver stepped on it. We thot[400] we lost them but no they had found our trail."

> "We shot up a little street which happened to be a blind alley. We crawled down the bottom until we past their car. When we reached mother's their car was there. So we drove past (sic) and parked by the Hospital. The Driver walked back and couldn't see their car, so drove us to mother's. We dressed in the dark because the kids were watching the house. Tom Rice picked us up, but they followed. We drove through the park near some bushes.[401] Then we 3 lost them. In the Hudson coach were Gladys, George Koch, Jack Riegger. Practically most of them that were in our bridal party. We stayed at the Chancellor Hotel on Powell Street the first night. They had phoned all the other hotels to see if we were registered there."

The Honeymoon.

Rose and Bob's honeymoon lasted 11 days:

> "October 15, 1925 we drove to Santa Rosa and spent the second night there. The next morning (we) drove to Sacramento. Stayed there a week. Drove all around the town. Wanted to go to Lake Tahoe but the roads were closed being so late in the season. Stopped a day and night at Stockton"

> "Had one glorious honeymoon."

---

[400] Original spelling.

[401] Buena Vista Park which was across the street from the Nimmo home.

10
THE TRIP EAST – 1927

"Stayed up to midnight myself last night putting pictures of people into Ancestry so now the family tree has faces. I thought those people shouldn't be faceless if I could give them a face." Beth Koller Whittenbury – Rose's Granddaughter

Times were tough after Bob and Rose married. About two weeks after their honeymoon, Bob fell ill, and Rose went back to work at the Neville Book Company.[402] Instead of living by themselves in a cozy apartment as they had planned, Bob and Rose first moved in with Bob's parents at 947 Noe.[403] Then they moved in with Rose's parents at 485 Buena Vista.[404] [405]

But, by 1927 things were looking up. Bob was working with his father

---

[402] "U.S. City Directories, 1822-1995. (San Francisco, San Francisco, California, 1926) *Ancestry.com* database entry for Rose Engelhardt. (Note: Rose Engelhardt is now a "typist" for Neville Books.)

[403] "U.S. City Directories, 1822-1995. (San Francisco, San Francisco, California, 1926) *Ancestry.com* database entry for Robert Engelhardt.

[404] "U.S. City Directories, 1822-1995." (San Francisco, San Francisco, California, 1927) *Ancestry.com* database entry for Robert Engelhardt.

[405] Story as told by Janice Engelhardt Koller to Barbara Hunter: When Bob became ill, Rose and Bob had to give up their apartment. Then, Bob and Rose initially lived upstairs in the Engelhardt's home, but it didn't work out as Bob's mother was too upset by the situation to be effectively supportive.

as a watchmaker.[406] And, it seems, both the Engelhardt and the Nimmo families banded together to give the couple a boost. That is, both families made it possible for Bob and Rose to take a splendid trip back east- first to Detroit to visit Rose's relatives and then onward to San Antonio, Texas to visit Bob's family.

It was such a memorable trip that Rose created a hand-made book about it which she called "The Trip East - 1927."[407] [408]

Bob and Rose left late Saturday night, August 13, 1927, on the Santa Fe[409] and arrived in Detroit, Tuesday, 7 p.m., August 16, 1927. Although they were heading for Detroit where Rose's grandmother, Marion Kerr Chalmers Nimmo, lived, the train first took them south to Arizona and New Mexico before they turned north through Oklahoma and Kansas to Chicago, Illinois. They reached Chicago by 10:30 a.m. on Tuesday, the 16th. There must have been a long stopover in Chicago because Rose and Bob finally reached Detroit almost 8 hours later. They were met at the Detroit train station by Rose's Aunt Marion, Rose's Uncle Alec and Marion's friend, Sadie Burgess.[410] [411]

***

---

[406] "U.S. City Directories, 1822-1995. (San Francisco, San Francisco, California, 1927) *Ancestry.com* database entry for Robert Engelhardt.

[407] Engelhardt, Rose Marion Nimmo. *The Trip East – 1927.* (Unpublished book) In possession of Beth Koller Whittenbury.

[408] All quotes about the trip in this chapter, unless otherwise specified, are Rose's words from *The Trip East- 1927*. The original spelling and grammar have been retained.

[409] The "Santa Fe" is the name of a train – which, these days, everyone might not know about.

[410] Sadie Burgess is Aunt Marion's "chum." Sadie, who was not married, was living in Detroit with her sister's family. In: "United States Census, 1930." *FamilySearch.org* database entry for Sadie Burgess.

[411] Both Marion and Sadie appear to be very active participants in most of Bob and Rose's activities during the 1927 visit. It seems, from Rose's comments in *The Trip East- 1927* that Marion and Sadie enjoyed Bob and Rose's visit - at least as much as Bob and Rose did - starting right away with meeting Bob and Rose at the Detroit train station.

By 1927, it had been over 40 years since the Nimmos had immigrated from Canada to Detroit. Rose's grandfather, **Thomas Nimmo**, after working as a machinist and a tool maker in Detroit for about 15 years, had died in Detroit on May 16, 1903.[412] He was 58.

However, Rose's **"Little Grandma," Marion Kerr Chalmers Nimmo**, still lived in her Detroit home at 5027 - 24th Street.[413] [414] Three of Rose's 6 aunts and uncles, Mary, Alexander and Marion, had remained in the Detroit, Michigan area.

Rose's **Aunt Mary Nimmo Scott**, the oldest Nimmo daughter, had married William Henry Scott, a Canadian from Ontario, on the 19th of March 1895 in Detroit. In 1927, the Scotts still lived in the Detroit area and had two grown children, Thomas Truman Scott and Marion Scott. Rose's cousin, **Tom Scott**, was 30 years old at the time of Rose and Bob's visit. He was married to **Gladys** Elizabeth Green. **Cousin Marion** Scott, who was married to Frank Gordon Schaub, was in the hospital at the time of the visit.

Uncle Alexander Hughey Nimmo had married **Mertie** McCloe on the 25th of June, 1913. They had a daughter, **Virginia**, on December 1, 1916. By 1927, **Cousin Virginia** was 10 years old. **Uncle Alex** was an electrician, and had his own business, A. H. Nimmo Electric Co..[415] [416]

---

[412] The 3 younger children, Alexander, Jean and Marion, were still living at their home (1285 – 24th) when their father, Thomas Nimmo, died. Alexander and Marion were just 20. Jean was 23. All of them were working but probably not earning enough to support all the members of the family that were still at home.

[413] This may have been a smaller house than when Thomas Nimmo was alive and all the unmarried children lived at home, that is, when the Nimmos lived at 1285- 24th in Detroit. In: "U.S. City Directories, 1822-1995." (Detroit, Michigan, City Directory, 1893.) *Ancestry.com* database entry for Marion Nimmo.

[414] "United States Census, 1930." *Ancestry.com* database entry for Marion Chalmers Nimmo.

[415] Alexander Hughey Nimmo, Rose's Uncle Alec, was born in Arthur, Canada on May 16, 1882. He was 45 years old at the time of the visit, about 21 years older than his niece, Rose. *The Book of Detroiters*, published in 1914, said he was unmarried (in 1914), resided in Detroit since 1888, was an electrical contractor and one of the people who organized the firm of Nimmo, Spaulding and Eddy in 1910 and was currently (at the time *The Book of Detroiters* was published in

Aunt Marion Chalmers Nimmo,[417] the youngest living child of Thomas and Marion Kerr Chalmers Nimmo, lived with her mother. Like her brothers and sisters, Aunt Marion had gone to work at an early age. By the age of 17, Marion, along with her sister, Jean, was working at the Michelle Table Supply Company.[418] From then on, Aunt Marion continued to work and to support her mother. She was the only child left at home when Rose and Bob came to visit. She "paled" with her good "Chum," **Sadie Burgess**.

Although three of the Nimmo siblings had stayed in Detroit, by 1927 the other three of Rose's aunts and uncles had married and moved elsewhere.

Uncle David Chalmers Nimmo remained a Canadian at heart. After spending a couple of years in Detroit when the family initially immigrated to the United States, it appears that David Nimmo returned to Ontario.[419]

However, in 1903, when his father died, David returned to Detroit where he remained until about 1925. It must be supposed that he took on the responsibilities of supporting his mother and his younger siblings who were not yet independent. During his many years in Detroit, David worked as a machinist, but he also received recognition as an author and a poet. He was a very active member of the Michigan Authors Association, and, for many years, he was their corresponding secretary.[420]

1914) its treasurer.

[416] By the 1927 visit, Uncle Alec was so successful that he had a Cadillac Sedan which he generously loaned to Bob and Rose. Therefore, on Wednesday, August 17, as Rose reports, Bob and Rose were able to start sight-seeing.

[417] Aunt Marion Chalmers Nimmo was never married and, it appears, always lived with and supported her mother. In: "United States Census, 1930." *FamilySearch.com* database entry for Marion C. Nimmo. In 1927, when Bob and Rose came to visit, Aunt Marion would have been about 45 years old – about 20 years older than Rose.

[418] "U.S. City Directories, 1822-1995." (Detroit, Michigan, City Directory, 1899) *Ancestry.com* database entry for Marion Chalmers Nimmo.

[419] Newspaper article describe David Nimmo as living in Toronto and visiting his family in Detroit. In: *Detroit Free Press*, 3 Oct 1897, Pp. 19. *Newspapers.com* database entry for David Nimmo.

[420] *Detroit Free Press*, 11 May 1919. Pp. 54. *Newspapers.com* database entry

In 1925, at the age of 59, Uncle David Chalmers Nimmo, married **"Lotte,"** Charlotte Elizabeth Klinck, in Toronto, and the couple was still living there in 1927.[421] [422]

In 1927, **Uncle Thomas Nimmo, Jr.** was living in the Los Angeles area with his wife, **Phoebe** Neuman Nimmo. Their only child, **Violet**, was living with her husband, Donald Macmillan in Sanel, California.[423]

Aunt Jean D. Nimmo Alexander married **Oscar** F. Alexander in 1903, just a few short months after the death of her father. The Alexanders lived in Cleveland, Ohio with their only child, **Charles D. Alexander**. Charles was born in 1908 which made him about 5 years younger than his cousin, Rose.[424]

***

---

for David Nimmo.

[421] David Chalmers Nimmo, the oldest of Thomas and Marion Nimmo's children, married "Aunt Lottie," Charlotte Elizabeth Klinck, in Toronto, Canada, on the 27th of June, 1925. At the time of their marriage, David was living at 5027 Twenty Fourth St, Detroit, Michigan, and Lottie was living at 2 Sherwood Ave. North Toronto. In their marriage record, David is a 59-year-old bachelor, and Lottie is a 57-year-old spinster. In: "Ontario, Canada Marriages, 1801-1928." *Ancestry.com* database entry for David Nimmo. David and Lottie had only been married for 2 years when Bob and Rose came to visit.

[422] David is a poet and a writer, and there are several newspapers articles that indicate that he was well-known in Detroit and active in literary organizations.

[423] Violet and Donald Macmillan are in Sanel, California by the 1930 United States Census. It does not appear that Violet and Donald Macmillan ever had children.

[424] Charles D. Alexander became a physician and remained single. He died in 1958 at the age of 49.

The Trip East – 1927[425]
(all in Rose's words and original spelling and grammar)

Our Trip East – August 1927

"Left late Saturday night August 12th on the Santa Fe.
Ate a lovely lunch and dinner mother Engelhardt fixed for (us) on August 13th.

Sunday ate	Breakfast	at	Gallup, Arizona
	Lunch	at	Bellue, New Mexico
	Dinner	at	Vaughn, New Mexico
Monday -	Breakfast	at	Wayaha, Oklahoma
	Lunch	at	Wellington, Kansas
	Dinner	at	Topeka, Kansas

Tuesday ate breakfast in the diner that we picked up just before we got to Chicago

> Arrived in Chicago at 10:30
> Reached Detroit Tuesday 7 p.m. August 16th

The train stopped at …Harvey house(s) for meals.
Aunt Marion, Uncle Alec, and Sadie met us when we arrived in Detroit at 7 p. m."

---

[425] Engelhardt. Rose Marion. *The Trip East – 1927*. Unpublished manuscript. In possession of Beth Koller Whittenbury. (Note: most original punctuation and spelling has been retained unless the punctuation or spelling caused too much confusion.)

Rose, Little Grandma Nimmo,
and Bob. Detroit. 1927.
Courtesy of Beth K. Whittenbury

Aunt Mary Nimmo Scott and
Grandma Marion Nimmo.
Detroit, Michigan. 1927.
Courtesy of Beth K. Whittenbury

Wednesday, August 17

"Uncle Alec loaned us his Cadillac sedan and Bob drove. Went to Bell Isle, Saw Scot's monument (beautiful fountain). Drove to...... Grosse pointe where the lovely mansions are."

"That night Alec, Sadie, Marion and we met cousins Tom and Gladys. Had dinner at Tuller's Hotel. Danced on black and white marble floor. Later went to Michigan Theater. Gorgeous. Tom and Gladys took us for a spin in their Chrysler Sedan then to Grandmas."[426]

---

[426] Although not specifically stated in Rose's book, Bob and Rose almost certainly stayed with "Little Grandma Nimmo" at her home on 24th Street. Grandma Nimmo was almost 82 years old at the time of Rose's visit. Aunt Marion was the only one of "Grandma Nimmo's" children still living at home so there must have been plenty of room in Grandma's house for Bob and Rose.

Rose Nimmo Engelhardt, Tom Scott (Rose's cousin) and his wife Gladys Green Scott. Detroit, Michigan. 1927. (Note: The houses in the background would have been typical of the Nimmo house in Detroit.) Courtesy of Beth Koller Whittenbury.

Thursday, August 18

"Went to hospital to see Cousin Marion. Poor dear, very ill. Later they took us to a Big League Ball game, but it rained. That night went to see play "Broadway." Swell show. Rained continuously. Had dinner with grandma who is such a dear."

Friday, August 19

"Bob, Marion & I went down to Hudson Fur Factory. Tried on $4 ($400) and $500 coats. Bought a lovely brown one for considerably less. Had lunch with Sadie Burgess (Marion's Chum) at the Women's City Club. Then met Tom and Gladys and saw Detroit play Boston double header."

"Alec called for that evening at grandma's and took us to dinner at the Detroit Yacht club. Simply marvelous beyond words. Went for a walk down the long wharf far out looking at the beautiful yachts. Had our first taste of frog legs."

Saturday, August 20[427]

"Uncle Alec picked us up at 1.30 p.m. to drive us to Lake Wamplers - a resort outside of Detroit. We passed through Fordson, Clinton, Dearborn, Ypsilanti. Arrived there 3:30 p.m. Had dinner with Aunt Mertie and cousin Virginia. Danced and Bowled that evening."

Uncle Alec, Cousin Virginia, Aunt Mertie Nimmo with Bob and Rose at Lake Norvell. 1927. Courtesy of Beth Koller Whittenbury.

Sunday, August 21

"Spent most the day riding on the lake. Had lots to talk about. Had breakfast, lunch and dinner at the Farm Hotel. Arrived back in Detroit 10:30 p. m."

Monday, August 22

"Sadie, Marion and we went to Bob-lo - 1 ½ hour ride on the Detroit river to the mouth of Lake Erie. Blanc Bois is the real name. It is a Canadian Park run by Americans. We rode on the whip, Merry-go-round and danced. Arrived back in Detroit at 8 p.m. That night took double-decker bus for the thrill of seeing the sights."

Tuesday, August 23

"Took 9 a.m. boat for Tashmoo. It is a 3 hour boat ride. Right after we got on the Island it poured, so we had to seek shelter. Ate lunch, played cards and danced a little. Glady, Tom, Marion and we caught the 6 p.m. boat. Ate dinner aboard. Arrived in Detroit at 9 p.m."

---

[427] On Saturday, probably Uncle Alec's day off, he took Bob and Rose to Lake Wamplers where Alec's wife, Mertie McCloe Nimmo, and his daughter, Virginia, were enjoying a summer vacation at a resort.

Wednesday, August 24 *(Suddenly, Rose and Bob's train tickets needed to be "fixed" because Rose's Uncle Dave and Aunt Lottie, who were living in Toronto, had just given Bob and Rose a "lovely trip" from Detroit to Toronto, Buffalo, Niagara Falls, Cleveland and back to Detroit.)*

"Marion helped Bob & I get our tickets fixed. Then Bob left with Alec and Tom to see the Ball Game. Ate his diner down town and saw Burlesque show. I spent the day with Marion and Gladys. Had a lovely luncheon engagement at Sadie's who has several other guests. Played bridge. In the evening went to the Beautiful Michigan Theater again. Lovely day."

Thursday, August 25

"Left Detroit at 4:40 p.m. A tearful farewell to little Grandma Nimmo and all our friends and relatives. Took train for Toronto. Passed thru Windsor. Arrived in Toronto 12:20 past midnight. Uncle Dave met us. Hired a limousine and took us to his home."

Uncle Dave Nimmo and Aunt Lottie Klinck Nimmo. Niagara Falls, New York. 1927. Courtesy of Beth Koller Whittenbury.

Friday, August 26

"Aunt Lottie, Uncle Dave, Aunt Marion and Sadie and we went down town to see some of Toronto. Visited Eastons department store. Covers 4 square blocks. Enormous. Had lunch on 9th floor in the Georgian Room – delicious. Then went back to the house."

"A limousine called for us and drove us all around Toronto. Saw Sunnyside (a coney (sic) island) Saw Casa Loma. Went in it, a huge castle. The owner went broke building it so now it is used as a hotel. Beautiful. Saw House of Parliament, old and new Buildings. Also Toronto College, very large. Saw exclusive Rosedale district. Also new arch for the Canadian exhibition and the buildings for the exposition."

Saturday, August 27

"Caught the 7:45 boat Cayuga from Toronto. On Lake Ontario 3 hours. Very rough. Many people sick. Passed inspection at Lewiston, New York by immigration authority."

"Took the Great Gorge trip through the whirlpool rapids. Arrived in Niagara Falls at 10:30 a.m. standard time.[428] Had lunch. Took small boat called "Maid of Mist" to see the bottom of Falls. Had to don oil skins to keep dry. Saw falls from all angles."

Aunt Lottie and Uncle Dave with Rose, Aunt Marion and Sadie Burgess. Niagara Falls, New York. 1927. Courtesy of Beth Koller Whittenbury.

Rose on the "Maid of the Mist" seeing Niagara Falls from all angles. 1927. Courtesy of Beth Koller Whittenbury.

---

[428] It is clear that "everyone" went to Niagara Falls. That is, along with Bob and Rose, Uncle Dave and Aunt Lottie and Aunt Marion and Sadie Burgess are pictured in front of the fence guarding the precipice of Niagara Falls.

"Took car over the bridge to Canadian side. While there Bob had some real beer as U.S. had prohibition. We had some sandwiches. Took Train to Buffalo, N.Y. Got on boat at Buffalo at 8 p.m. for Cleveland. One wonderful day. Will never forget those sights."

Sunday, August 28

"Cousin Charles met us.[429] Drove us to his house for breakfast. After that took us for a long drive to show us Cleveland. That night took us to Allen's Theater to see Clara Bow in "Hula Hula.""

Aunt Jean (Nimmo) and Uncle Oscar Alexander and son Charles (Chuck). Cleveland, Ohio. 1927. Courtesy of Beth Koller Whittenbury.

Monday, August 29

"Went down to see the stores. Went through Highies- Lindners- Halls

---

[429] Cousin Charles is Charles Alexander. Bob and Rose are in Cleveland to visit the Alexanders: Aunt Jean D. Nimmo Alexander, Uncle Oscar Alexander and their son, Charles Alexander. Jean D. Nimmo Alexander is George Nimmo's sister and the 5th living child of Thomas and Marion Nimmo. Oscar F. Alexander, is a carpenter/contractor, who seems to have always lived in Cleveland, Ohio. In 1927, Cousin Charles would have been 18- just a bit too young to go nightclubbing with Bob and Rose.

and others. Monday afternoon drove around. Went to Euclid Beach at night. Took in concessions and danced. Had dinner out."

Tuesday, August 30

"Went down town and through Keith's Palace. Marvelous place. Left Cleveland on the City of Cleveland III at 11:30 p.m. Uncle Oscar took us to a marvelous dinner miles out in the country where we ordered anything and everything we wanted."

Wednesday, August 31

"Arrived back in Detroit at 7 A.M. Had breakfast at Grandma Nimmo's. Marion had to go to her office in the morning. Sadie met me and we shopped. Then took me to the Buick-Cadillac Hotel. Very beautiful Hotel. Then we took several bus lines and saw more of Detroit. That evening went to the hospital to say good-bye to cousin Marion. Then Tom and Gladys drove us out to Auntie McVities.[430] (She's dad's Aunt nearly 80 years old.) Thence home."

Thursday Sept 1st

"Went to town to have my hair shampooed and waved. Met Gladys, took cab home, them packed trunk. At 1 p.m. Tom called for us and took us to a "blind pig" for lunch. Then took up for a ride to Palmer Park and Bloomfield Hills, (exclusive residential districts). Uncle Alec came out after dinner and we all chatted."

Friday September 2

"Jean, Charles and Uncle Oscar long-distanced from Cleveland to tell us good bye. Tom Scott was to drive us to depot but was late so Marion called us a cab. Sadie met us at the depot. Tom got there just as we were leaving."

Farewell Detroit

***

One can imagine the confusion and consternation when Tom Scott

---

[430] This is Grandma Marion Kerr Chalmers Nimmo's sister, Agnes Chalmers McVittie.

fails to show up to take Bob and Rose to the train station. But Rose, as always, seemed to manage these little difficulties and to board the train to Texas with a sense of perspective and calm.

In fact, throughout her life Rose Marion Nimmo Engelhardt was always enthusiastic, loving and supportive. Her ability to navigate and survive many difficult times was due to her innate moral values and her determined spirit - some of which she got from her tough, resilient, hard-working immigrant ancestors – some of which was just who she was.

In 1927, at the age of 24, Rose had much of her family story ahead of her - which must be saved for another book. But, as we close these chapters of Rose's family history, we can reflect on a quote from Rose, which was initially meant for her husband, Bob, but which she, with her indomitable spirit, would have meant for everyone she loved, "...buck up, and let's forget the troubles of the past, and stake our love and happiness on the future." [431]

"And they lived happily ever after . . ." Beth Koller Whittenbury – Rose's Granddaughter

"I wonder what these relatives would think about us all caring about their lives. I wonder if future generations will look at us and wonder too." Sue Arden West – Rose's Granddaughter

---

[431] Unpublished letter from Rose to Bob, 1926. In possession of Dolores Jean Engelhardt Arden.

EPILOGUE
REMEMBERING ROSE

"I loved every moment I got to spend with her." Nancy Arden Cummins, Rose's Granddaughter.

"My memories are simple, loving & sweet – it is always the small stuff of the heart that really means so much too." Sue Arden West, Rose's Granddaughter

"Oh – such great memories." Beth Koller Whittenbury, Rose's Granddaughter

Barbara Hunter, Rose's niece. Rose Marion Nimmo Engelhardt was a special person. Everyone loved and admired her. She was principled, steadfast and courageous as well as loving and supportive.

My mother, Helene Engelhardt Hunter was Rose's sister-in-law. The Hunter and Engelhardt families were always very close. We went often to visit my Aunt Rose, my Uncle Bob and my two cousins, Dolores (Doll) and Janice (Jannie). Every time we arrived for a visit, Rose, Doll and Jannie would stream from the front door, with Rose in the lead, arms wide to give everyone a big hug. Rose's happiness at simply seeing us always made us feel very loved.

At some point in our visits, Rose would say, "Let's all gather around the piano and sing." (Remember, Rose and Bob loved to sing together.) This was somewhat alarming because no one in our family had inherited the lovely Engelhardt voice, and none of us could sing a note. We also didn't know any of the songs Rose loved so – they seemed to me to be songs from the 30's – but I'm really not sure. However, I remember Rose standing, one hand on the piano, gripping her sheet music, and bursting enthusiastically into song.

However, there were lots of hard bumps along the way. One of the worst was when Bob Engelhardt (Rose's Bobby Dear) and my father, Louis Marion Hunter, died on the same day – September 21, 1958. In separate circumstances and locations, they had died of heart attacks. The families were devastated. But Rose gathered her daughters, and, amid the devastation, drove over to my mother's home to check on and support our family.

Two years later, when I was18, Rose and her daughter, Jan, made sure I knew how to register and enroll in college. They realized my mother really had no experience upon which to draw - so they stepped in. Despite the fact that both families were struggling financially, Rose and Jan gave me an envelope full of money ($50) to cover the cost of books for my first semester. That was a fortune at the time. Rose also gave me the key to her home which was near my college. She said that days at college were long and that, even though she was working, I was free to use her home, eat any of her food, and sleep in her bed if I needed to take a nap.

My Aunt Rose was always a terrific support to me. I remember her with such love and gratitude.

Dolores Engelhardt Arden (Doll), Rose and Bob's Daughter
Memories of my mother, Rose, whom I always called "mommie:"

She was unselfish, loving, caring, generous, friendly, humble, modest, thrifty, helpful and fun.

I was born at the start of the depression so there never was a lot of money, but both mommie and daddy never let us feel deprived. I had a happy childhood.

One of the favorite and popular expressions she used was "come over for coffee and.........." - meaning whenever family or friends came over, mommie would provide coffee AND whatever little treat they could share with the visitors.

She was not a fancy cook, but we had good healthy meals. One of our special favorites was pineapple upside down cake - whenever she pulled out the cast iron skillet, we knew we would get the special treat of a delicious upside down cake complete with the red cherries on top.

She would give us sweet but simple and fun birthday parties with games and decorations.

In high school, I had several formal dresses, and she remade one or two, and they were special. For high school graduation, there were several activities, and she thought I needed extra outfits so she worked it out for me to have them.

Whenever she rode a bus or street car, she would always chat with her fellow passengers.

She often would take the streetcar in San Francisco to the terminal and then take the bus over the Bay Bridge to Walnut Creek to visit me and her granddaughters (Nancy and Sue). I would pick her up at the terminal, and we would spend the day before her return to San Francisco.

My dear Aunt Helene (Barbara's mom) and mommie were dear friends and enjoyed being together. They took a trip to Texas together to see relatives there. Later they and my dad took a trip to Disneyland. My mommie wanted to buy a pair of slacks to wear but was hesitant to do so as she always wore dresses and wondered how she would look. I talked her into buying a pair of slacks, and she looked great.

When my daddy and Barbara's dad passed away on the same day, both mommie and Aunt Helene showed how courageous they were and found jobs and went back to work. Mommie would take a streetcar and bus to work. Shortly thereafter she relearned to drive and bought herself a car and then her transportation was easier.

After she passed on, one of the things that I missed the most was not being able to phone her and tell her of an exciting event that had happened that day. She loved hearing things that went on.

I am so blessed growing up to have had such a dear mother, father, and sister, Jannie, and also for all the dear relatives that have joined the family along the way.

Janice Marion Engelhardt Koller (Jannie), Rose and Bob's Daughter

Jan was Rose and Bob's youngest daughter. She passed on much too soon. She was a prolific and dedicated writer and would have loved to help write this book.

Jan's loving spirit is still very present in this book. Her daughter, Beth Koller Whittenbury, incorporated some of Jan's writing into Chapter 6, "Rose – Early Years" which was based on stories Rose told Jan about the Nimmo Family and their life in San Francisco.

Nancy Arden Cummins, Rose and Bob's Granddaughter

I remember Grandma Rose used to take my sister and I on walks down the back ally way, across 19th Avenue, down a steep long set of stairs to a yummy bakery. She'd buy us shortbread cookies, and they were carefully put into a pink box tied with twine to take home. But she'd always get us a cookie to eat at the bakery.

I remember getting on the street car to ride to the zoo or to the shopping center down 19th Avenue with her.

Grandma Rose was the only one that I would let cut my bangs. My mom would cut them too short, but Grandma always tried to cut them to the eyebrow, which made me very happy.

Grandma Rose made the best fruit salad for special occasions. It had fruit cocktail and frozen strawberries. She would spoon it into beautiful crystal stem glasses. It felt so fancy. Today I have those crystal stem glasses. I made her recipe when my kids were little but never seemed as special.

Grandma Rose taught us how to play Bunco. She was always patient when we played.

She had a great set of Nancy Drew books that's she'd let me read and they smelled old and musty...a great smell memory.

I remember her big warm hugs while wearing a big apron. She was a good cook! She always loved us to visit any time...she was a special lady...

Elizabeth Koller Whittenbury (Beth), Rose and Bob's Granddaughter

I remember my Grandma Rose with such love and affection! She essentially raised me for the first few years of my life and took care of my mother at the same time. As it was described to me, she always took in and nursed family members who needed it, starting with her own mother, then her niece Phyllis for a time, and then my mother and me. Since I spent so much time in her house, I remember it fairly well, even though I was pretty little. When I would visit, she would take me across 19th Ave. to the shopping center where there was a bakery. She would buy me a cookie there in the shape of a leaf. I loved those leaf cookies mostly because they were special times spent with Grandma. I believe they were shortbread with green icing that made the leaf pattern. They weren't very big, but they were yummy. Grandma would always grab my hand when we crossed 19th avenue and taught me to look both ways before crossing even though we did it in a cross walk and at a stop light. I always felt she cared for me and was looking out for me.

During visits, I would stay in her guest room upstairs. On the wall of that room were two pictures of ballerinas in pink "Tootoos." I was completely enthralled with those "Tootoos," even though I wasn't a very good ballerina myself. I couldn't point my toe enough and I wasn't limber at all. So, I didn't follow Grandma's natural ability in that area. However, she knew I loved the costumes, so she would often sew me ballerina costumes and many "Tootoos" for me out of netting she would get at the fabric store. She had taught my mom how to sew, and I wore mostly hand sown clothes throughout my early elementary school days and even some into college. Grandma tried to teach me a bit, but I was still too little to be trusted with the sewing machine when she was still here. However, she taught my mom and my mom later taught me, so I assumed that sewing and dancing just ran in the family. Grandma also got me started on samplers. She had samplers that she had made hanging throughout her house and I grew up thinking that was the standard wall hanging in houses.

It became our little special custom to go see the City of Paris Christmas Tree[432] every year in celebration of our respective birthdays which both fell at the end of November. I remember the awe I felt when I first saw that tree and asking her how they got it in there. She explained that they took the roof off and lowered the live tree down by a crane every year. I really miss that tree and that special time with her. We would also go see the displays in all the department store windows on Union Square. In those days they were really something - always animated and magical.

I don't remember ever hearing a cross word from Grandma Rose, although now I realize that she must have been dealing with a lot. I never saw her treat anyone other than with love and respect. She loved Christian Science and would talk with me about it. She had a testimony about a physical healing published in the *Christian Science Sentinel*. She really expressed the unconditional love that forms the basis of that religion.

I remember her talking, at times, about her late husband, Grandpa Bob, with tremendous affection in her voice. She related stories about his sense of humor. Her tone made it clear that he had been her great love.

In sum, I remember my grandmother was the most loving, giving person I've ever encountered. I always felt safe, valued, secure and loved when I was with her. I remember my mother telling me once that she had found a letter written to Rose by one of her school friends in which she described Rose as an angel. That's how I think of her too and can only hope I've grown up to make her proud.

Susan Arden West (Sue), Rose and Bob's Granddaughter

I remember Grandma's big smile and hug as we opened her front door to greet us. I felt very loved by Grandma. I remember her love & smile but also remember her as somewhat serious. I loved our visits. Grandma always had a pitcher of orange juice in her refrigerator and chocolate marshmallow cookies in pantry waiting for me. I loved nothing more than those special treats. We would sit down on her "nogahid" banquet in the kitchen and talk. I loved listening to the tick tock of her kitchen clock which I now have in my dining area.

I enjoyed staying overnight in her room. I slept in both the upstairs bedrooms at times. She always put a chair next to my bed so I wouldn't fall out of bed (even when I was 10). I remember her saying "Go get in your birthday suit" when she was running my bath. I was very young & it was

---

[432] The City of Paris was a department store in downtown San Francisco. The huge Christmas tree was installed in the rotunda of the store and must have been 3 stories tall.

the first time I heard that. We both laughed & laughed as I thought it was so funny.

During my visits, I would go to her third drawer down in kitchen next to the stove to get a wrinkled folded bag. We would then fill the bag with bread. I remember the drawer having a certain smell which I loved. I just loved doing this as it meant we were going to take the street car to Golden Gate Park to feed the ducks. She always tied a "lady" scarf around my head as she worried about the cold air in my ears. At the time I wasn't thrilled with that, but it is very sweet looking back. As we returned from Golden Gate Park we would stop at Stonestown Safeway & buy a cheese pizza – life was good. In the evening we played Bunco for long periods of time – such fun.

She also had a box upstairs in the landing that was filled with toys for us girls. There was Sootie (a puppet) & a English spaniel book which had the dogs dressed & interacting as people. Just loved that book.

When visiting for family dinners, we would have celery with pimento cheese spread inside. I would help her spread the cheese. We would bring out the appetizers to the group in the living room all gathered in a circle. Frequently, we would play the piano & sing. I remember Auntie Jan playing & singing along with Grandma.

Grandma came to visit us in Walnut Creek a few times. I know it was a very long trip so she didn't come often. Nancy & I loved to swim and play on the bars in our back lot. As much as Grandma tried, she just couldn't watch us as it made her quite nervous so stayed in the house. I remember the day she put on a swimsuit & went in the water for a moment. Auntie Jan taught me to swim in our pool. I remember that so well - like it was yesterday.

I know that Auntie Helen and Grandma were besties. They would laugh long and loud when they were together. Grandma passed on when I was 15 years old. I am so grateful I felt so loved by my grandma. My last memory of her is standing at her front gate of the white picket fence on Thanksgiving waving good-bye and blowing us all a kiss.

***

"One generation's love, support and courage is the foundation upon which the lives of the next generation are built." Barbara Lorraine Hunter, Rose's Niece

The Children, Grandchildren, Great Grandchildren and Great-Great Grandchildren of Rose Marion Nimmo and Robert Caspar Engelhardt

Children:	Dolores Jean
	Janice Marion
Grandchildren:	Nancy Jean
	Susan Joan
	Elizabeth Rose
Great Grandchildren:	Joshua Charles
	Jeffrey Robert
	Sara Emily
	Kyle Andrew
	William Arthur
Great, Great Grandchildren:	Mac Leland
	Brayden Grant

May all of you continue to be blessed by Rose's loving spirit and her generous heart.

Barbara Lorraine Hunter
May 1, 2018

ABOUT THE AUTHOR

Barbara Hunter has held a wide variety of interesting jobs. She has sold tickets for roller coaster rides at San Francisco's Playland-at-the-Beach and has been the Assistant Director of the Oregon Employment Department.

Currently, she is trying to scale genealogical "brick walls" in search of elusive ancestors. She also paints at her studio which is located just south of Salem, Oregon. She shows her paintings in the local Salem/Keizer area.

She can be contacted at hunterbl1@comcast.net.

www.ingramcontent.com/pod-product-compliance
Lightning Source LLC
Chambersburg PA
CBHW050133280326
41933CB00010B/1355